The Tin Can Crucible

THE
TIN CAN
CRUCIBLE

A FIRSTHAND ACCOUNT
OF MODERN-DAY SORCERY VIOLENCE

CHRISTOPHER
DAVENPORT

LUME BOOKS
A JOFFE BOOKS COMPANY

LUME BOOKS
A JOFFE BOOKS COMPANY

First published in 2020 by Lume Books
30 Great Guildford Street,
Borough, SE1 0HS

ISBN 978-1-83901-219-8

Typeset using Atomik ePublisher from Easypress Technologies

www.lumebooks.co.uk

About the Author

Christopher Davenport is a Foreign Service Officer with the U.S. Department of State. He has served tours in Vietnam, Guatemala, Washington DC, Tajikistan, and the Eastern European nation of Georgia. He has also worked in Albania, Moldova, and Bosnia and Herzegovina.

His first international experience was as a Peace Corps Volunteer in Papua New Guinea from 1994 to 1996. His time living in a village of subsistence farmers in the Papua New Guinean Highlands forms the basis of his memoir, *The Tin Can Crucible.* He and his wife have two daughters and an assortment of pets they have collected from around the world.

.

Wilt thou forgive that sin where I begun,
Which was my sin, though it were done before?
Wilt thou forgive that sin, through which I run,
And do run still, though still I do deplore?
When thou hast done, thou hast not done,
For I have more.

Wilt thou forgive that sin which I have won
Others to sin, and made my sin their door?
Wilt thou forgive that sin which I did shun
A year or two, but wallow'd in, a score?
When thou hast done, thou hast not done,
For I have more.

I have a sin of fear, that when I have spun
My last thread, I shall perish on the shore;
But swear by thyself, that at my death thy Son
Shall shine as he shines now, and heretofore;
And, having done that, thou hast done;
I fear no more.

'A Hymn to God the Father'
John Donne (1572–1631)

Foreword

The island nation of Papua New Guinea lies amid the blue-green waters of the South Pacific, close to the equator, a few hundred miles north of Australia. Its tranquil shores give way to a turbulent landscape, subject to earthquakes, mudslides, and volcanic eruptions. The land wanders beneath dense emerald rainforests that drape across a central range of towering mountains, known as the Highlands. Little towns nestle here and there among the mountain ranges, isolated from one another by long stretches of steep ridges and narrow valleys, but most of the inhabitants of the Highlands live in small villages, clusters of bush-material huts circled around central patches of cleared-out forest.

One of these is a place called Mari-eka. It is a collection of a dozen huts and carefully tended gardens in the Eastern Highlands province. It may or may not still be there today – Highland villages tend to be mobile, their locations determined by the uncertainties of land cultivation, hunting grounds, and tribal disturbances. But in December 1994, it was situated just outside the district capital of Goroka, a few miles off the Highlands Highway.

A few days before Christmas that year, warriors from Mari-eka raided a neighboring village and kidnapped two women, believing at least one of them to be a witch, who the villagers believed had killed an elder of their tribe. They forced the women back to Mari-eka, locked them in a hut, and accused them of the practice of sorcery. They threatened and bullied the captive women, demanding they confess. After days of abuse, one of the women could take no more, and she turned against the other. She said she knew the other woman was a witch and that she had used *sanguma*, black

i

magic, to take the elder's life. It was all the villagers needed to hear. They released the accuser, and they killed the woman who remained.

I know this, because I was living in the village at the time.

I had recently arrived in Papua New Guinea as a Peace Corps Volunteer, to spend two years teaching high school English at a mountain boarding school. But for my first few months, I lived in this tiny village on the edge of the world, with a family of subsistence farmers. There, in the moss-covered montane forest, amid the mud, rain, and cloud, I tried to learn their language and understand a little about their way of life.

This homestay was meant to be a waypoint of sorts, before I began my assignment – a chance to acclimate to the land I would call home for the next two years. Living in the village, sharing meals with the people there, spending evenings telling stories around the fire, sleeping in a bush-material home with my host family, would help me develop a sense of perspective on where the kids at my school had come from, what their home lives were like. The idea was that I would be better able to relate to my students once I had walked a mile in their shoes.

In fact, my time in the village would become more profound than anything I could ever have imagined. In those weeks, days, and hours, I witnessed the full scope of life and death. I saw benevolent kindness, endless generosity, dedication, and hope. I saw pageantry, ceremony, intimacy, and naked honesty. I saw the dignity, frailty, and grace of a people who seemed at harmony with one another, but at odds with the world around them. I watched the sun set on an old generation and rise before a new one. I saw fear, loss, rage, betrayal, and brutality. I saw the fullness of humanity in all its manifestations; all that we aspire to be and all we are afraid to recognize in ourselves.

And when I left, I knew that I would never be the same.

I knew, too, that what had happened during my time there was something that should be talked about. A story that needed to be told. I owed it to the people with whom I had lived – all of them, but especially the woman, the accused "sorceress," whose name I never even knew, but who has remained in my thoughts and memories ever since.

After I finished my volunteer assignment and returned to the States, I began writing a verbatim transcript of my journal entries from those days in the village. It began as a jumbled mess of handwritten notes scrawled by the light of nothing more than the dim, flickering glow of a kerosene lantern in my Highland village. Years later, back home, it was difficult for me to make any sense of what I had written there. The scattered, nearly illegible impressions were like Rorschach inkblots, indistinct shapes and forms that, put together, suggested insights I couldn't have accurately described at the time. I had been so close to what was happening, and it was all happening so quickly, it was impossible at the time for me to have any perspective, or to make any sense of it. It took years to draw it together.

So, years passed. I wrote, and I waited, I suppose, for answers. How could this have happened? How could the people I lived with– who looked out for me, cared for me, worried over me, offered to share with me everything they possessed– do something so final, so terrible, so unforgivable? For the remainder of my days in the village, the rest of my time in that country, and the years that have since passed, I have tried to find some insight, or at least explanation, in the cognitive dissonance I saw there. I have had to live for twenty-five years with what happened, with what they did, and what I failed to prevent.

Much as I wanted to, I couldn't bring myself to hate the people of the village for their actions. Despite the miracle of our technological advancements, our detailed accounting of thousands of years of human and social evolution, all the studied refinements of our philosophies, I couldn't convince myself I knew something they didn't. They were no more savage than the people who had "civilized" them decades before, and they were no more corrupt than I am.

But how could I tell the story without vilifying or demonizing the people of my village? How could I explain that, in spite of the outrage of what had happened there, in spite of what they had undeniably done, I still somehow felt the same sense of attachment and indebtedness to them, for all they had done for me, all they had taught me, all they had given me? No one had ever shared anything so precious with me. I didn't feel I had done anything to deserve the kindness they had shown me.

I felt like I had to earn it.

And now, when all has been said and done, and my time in the village is twenty-five years behind me, the only way for me to "earn it" is to try to tell their story as best I can. To be honest about who they were and what they meant to me, and to do right by her – and by them – by describing what happened there, a quarter of a century ago.

I hope that the people in these pages do not appear as mere cultural oddities – walking, talking archetypes of the bizarre and exotic. This not a tale of pure and unspoiled mountain tribespeople, and it is not an anthropological or sociological treatise. It is not an indictment of the beliefs and the way of life of the people who shared their lives with me for those days and weeks and months. If I have done my job, then the people in these pages are living, breathing men and women; complicated, sympathetic, but above all recognizable. And the things they felt and thought and did, right or wrong, were very real.

Christopher Davenport
January 2020

December 23, 1994 – Memory

What should become of the things we remember?

I remember crawling along the raw contours of the side of a mountain, inching forward on elbows and knees blackened with thick grains of damp soil. I remember the sun-warmed earth, and the way it perspired and exhaled beneath me. I remember running blistered fingertips along a yellow vine that disappeared into the mounds of dirt; prying at the ground with a machete, withdrawing a gnarled crop and heaping it to the side, drawing the back of my hand across my brow, feeling the sting of razor-thin cuts left on my wrist by the elephant grass that lined the mountain trail.

I remember the advance of darkening clouds across a low sky, and a vernal breeze that billowed through the valley. The way it brushed the sun from my back and animated the cedars and beeches, making them nod and sway. The drifting scents of wood smoke and pig manure. Birds of paradise shrieking in response to the calls of kingfishers and swallows. The dissonant birdsongs resounded from the steep ridges before suffocating in the damp air. The serrated mountains steeped in these echoing sounds, and in the stillness in between.

I remember straightening my back to stare across the field at Papa, who was working nearby. The two of us had hiked all morning to arrive at this garden and unearth its harvest – and now we stooped low over the erupted soil to fill our string bags, with only the silence between us.

Dwindling rays of sunshine pierced the clouds to find their way to his shoulders and radiate from the darkness of his skin. I watched him with the bewildering mixture of admiration and disdain, deference and contempt that seems only to exist within the indefinite boundaries of father and son.

But he wasn't my father. I called him "Papa," and he considered me his son, and during my time in the village we had created a façade of family and convinced everyone, including ourselves, that it was real. But we had met just a month before. And what had happened over the past few days had shown how little I knew him.

I couldn't believe what he'd done. The murder of an innocent woman. I would never know exactly what role he played in her death, whether he had contributed to the ending of her life with his own hands or merely consented to her destruction by the cruelty of others. It doesn't matter. He was complicit in what happened to her.

I took it personally, as any son would, as if it had something to do with me. I resented having to live with what he, and the people of the village, had done; having to couple their shame with my own and drape it across my shoulders like a wool blanket.

I wanted desperately to make sense of the sacrifice they had exacted, to somehow comprehend their compulsion to this act. I thought there might be some way to find absolution for my failure to stop them. I thought all of us could find a way to forgiveness.

Papa and I had barely spoken that morning. Days had passed since we'd had a normal conversation. I knelt in silence beside him that afternoon, pulling the pale crops from the failing grasp of a worried earth, as if rudely extricating interred bodies from their recent, unfinished burial.

I remember wondering where we would go from there.

November 17–18, 1994 – Paradise

I had traveled to Papua New Guinea from Wisconsin by way of San Francisco, where I joined the two dozen other volunteers who formed my Peace Corps group. We flew fifteen hours from San Francisco to Hong Kong, then raced across the airport concourse to meet our connecting flight, our bellies full of microwaved airplane food, warm beer and the boundless expectation of the newly converted. We flew seven more hours before landing in Port Moresby, Papua New Guinea, in the heart of the South Pacific. Here, we would recoup from jet lag, complete paperwork, start receiving immunizations and acclimate to the tropics.

Moresby, as the capital is called, is a febrile city of a quarter million souls. It seems to have been spilled accidentally amid the barren hillsides that ramble to the edges of the Gulf of Papua. Shore breezes drift inland from the Coral Sea to shudder the palm fronds, and the turquoise waters and lush pandanus appear as an idyll of tranquil repose. But up close, the palms are rotted and decayed, their trunks covered in graffiti. The window louvers of the dusty buildings are angled against the relentless sun, making the dwellings look as if they are squinting, grimacing. Cars and buses trace haphazard routes along the streets, and their oily exhaust mingles with the smoke from burning trash. Pedestrians shuffle warily along sidewalks scarred by razor wire and broken glass.

Moresby draws hopeful souls from villages throughout the country, who are lured there by tales of wealth and prosperity– but they find neither. The disillusioned migrants press into squatter settlements amid unforgiving heat and hopeless squalor. Crime and drugs are rampant, and the city

3

seethes with a quiet menace, agitated by hot breezes that suck breath from straining lungs.

Bound by yellowed grasslands and strewn with trash, Moresby is industrial and urban, but it's an illusion, like the ghostly mirages that rise from its sunbaked coastal flats. It doesn't seem real; and in a sense, it isn't.

The essence of the country lies inland, in its mountainous interior, known as the Highlands. The heart and soul of the land and of its people reside in the heights of its mountains and the enormity of its rainforests, which encroach through the shimmering heat to the edge of Moresby, as if poised to engulf it entirely, before petering out on the lowland flats.

The Highlands of Papua New Guinea remains one of the last truly wild places on Earth. Its inhabitants live in bush-material huts, without electricity or running water. They eat whatever they grow in their gardens, gather in the forest, or hunt with bow and arrow. They live a way of life that has changed little in thousands of years.

It was here that our in-country training would take place.

"Here's what'll happen," the Peace Corps country director's voice echoed from cinderblock walls as if resonating from a tin can, as fat blue flies droned around us. "You'll get inoculations here in Moresby, start on malaria preventatives and begin studying the language. Next week, you'll move up to the Highland town of Goroka. Each of you will stay in a village, with a traditional family. You'll share their chores and meals, sleep alongside them in their huts. Mornings, you'll come to the training center, where you'll learn about working and living in the community. Evenings, you go back to your families. You'll be the only Westerner in your village, so you're on your own, sink or swim. Any questions?"

There were plenty, but none of us had the courage to ask. We'd been told the Highlanders would be mesmerized by our pale skin, our peculiar habits, and our strange way of speaking. They anticipated the personification of all they'd heard of the West, from tales of Allied soldiers driving the Japanese from these same rainforests during World War II, to the B-grade action movies shown in crowded trade stores, powered by diesel generators.

I would never live up to their expectations. I was an ordinary kid from the American Midwest, a typical middle child who had spent his life trying to avoid the notice of parents, siblings, neighbors, teachers. There was nothing exotic or exceptional about me.

I was born in Tunkhannock, a tiny speck amid the coal and gas mines of eastern Pennsylvania. I spent my childhood roaming the expansive yards of the town's old Victorian homes, racing my bicycle over the cracked slate sidewalks. My friends and I would perch on the railway trestle that ran alongside the Grand Army of the Republic Highway and watch the eddies of the Susquehanna River drift beneath, our pale bare feet dangling above the creosote. We played tag in Gravel Hill Cemetery, racing across the graves of Civil War veterans and prominent residents from a bygone era. It was a step removed from a Norman Rockwell painting, and it was all we had ever known. We could barely conceive a world beyond it.

But when I was nine, my family moved to Green Bay, Wisconsin, a blue-collar city of farms and factories, a patchwork of dairy pastures, paper mills and warehouses. It was a city of Scandinavian propriety and Puritan guilt, where imposing red brick churches scowled at the smoke-filled bars on the other side of the streets. During summers, the town's eponymous bay festered with algae blooms, suffocating the walleye, perch, and carp and filling the town with the scent of decay. In winter, the waters iced over, the ground froze solid and the sun disappeared for months. It seemed unbearably frigid and insular after the dependable affability of the little town in Pennsylvania I had left behind.

My parents' divorce a few years later was relatively civil, but to my siblings and me, it was a trauma. Typically, we took our frustrations and disillusionments out on each other and everything around us. We acted up and acted out, got in trouble in school and at home. A shy child to begin with, I was unhappy with who I was and where I found myself, and I blamed Green Bay for it all.

My brothers, my sister and I gave little thought to anything aside from escaping the fetid waters and the smells of dead fish and cow manure. The disenchantment of our adolescence sat heaped around us amid banks of dirty snow. We each left as soon as we could, to scatter ourselves across the country.

I went to college in Ohio, because no one knew me there, and I thought I might leave behind the awkward kid I had been. I studied history and literature, the literal and metaphorical manifestations of a world far from my own, but I remained within a few hundred miles of where I was born and raised. The notion of a universe beyond the confines of the Midwest remained academic to me.

As I neared graduation, I took notice of ads for the Peace Corps, where idealistic volunteers worked alongside native farmers, turning the earth, feeding the crops, mending the fabric of society. The volunteers wore a look of implicit satisfaction at having found a calling. They seemed to exist in an entirely different reality from the cold winds and emotional turbulence that were all I had ever known.

I knew I couldn't just walk away from the person I had been or the things that had formed me. But I tried anyway. I joined the Peace Corps, and I told them I'd go wherever they sent me, however distant, however different.

They sent me to Papua New Guinea.

November 27, 1994 – Mountains

When the initial adjustments of our time in Moresby were behind us, I sat among the other volunteers aboard an Air Niugini turboprop, drifting over forested mountains, the passenger cabin occasionally shuddering as we flew through the pockets of warm air and humidity that rose from the shadowy jungle below. The confusion and heat of the capital faded as we ascended into the Highlands.

I sat in silence, unnerved by the uncertainty of what lay before me. I had never done anything like this, pushed myself so far afield. I had never sought to learn the stuff I was made of. And now, I was afraid of what I might find.

I knew almost nothing of this place. How would I relate to people so unlike me? Did I have the wherewithal to learn? What if it was too much for me?

A flight attendant handed me a plastic cup of mango cordial and a packet of stale sugar cookies, and I took them, though I wasn't hungry. I'd already learned that in this place, opportunity was as good a reason to eat as appetite. I took what was offered and watched our progress, as the propellers droned and the smeared window beside my seat trembled in its frame.

The landscape below seemed to rise to greet us, as if it were animated, spirited, uneasy. Jagged peaks, steep mountain slopes and dizzying valley walls tore through the delicate haze of cloud as though peering through a parted curtain. Despite the brutality of the scarred terrain, the trees, vines, and undergrowth encompassed everything, virtually unbroken, covering the surface in a thick cloak of emerald. The expanse of flora blanketed the land with colors so warm and vivid, the flowing ridges seemed almost to hum and pulse, like raised veins along living flesh.

7

Yet people lived down there, beneath that abundant canopy, amid the hopelessly tangled network of hills, rivers and mud. They descended from nomads who had crossed land bridges created by the lowered sea levels of an ancient ice age, the early Papua New Guineans settling there to remain in isolation for 60,000 years.

It wasn't until the sixteenth century that the outside world arrived at the island of New Guinea, in the form of Portuguese explorers. They named it *Ilhas dos Papuas*, or "Island of the Fuzzy Hairs," after the tight curls of the people they found there. The Spaniards came next and called it *Nueva Guinea*, noting a resemblance between the indigenous people and the dark-skinned natives of African Guinea.

For centuries, control of the region was determined by an imperial tug-of-war carried out among the empires of Portugal, Spain, Germany, Britain, and Japan. After World War II, eastern New Guinea became a mandated territory of the United Nations under the administration of Australia, while the western side was a far-flung province of Indonesia. Then, in 1975, the eastern mandate became the independent state of Papua New Guinea.

Its Melanesian inhabitants were tough, sturdy people with blunt features, wiry black hair, and coffee-brown skin. They were villagers and tribesmen, subsistence farmers and hunter-gatherers, inextricably tied to the land and to each other, fiercely loyal to tribe and family. The world beyond the visible horizon had little meaning to them, except as the formless ethereal realm inhabited by the spirits of their deceased ancestors.

I felt shrunken and humbled as I stared from the plane at this vibrant composite of plant, water, mud, and man, acutely aware of how far from my element I was. The notion that I had come here to help these people seemed almost laughable, when it was so plain that I would be the one who needed their help.

Our plane banked sharply to approach a concrete runway cut from the forest. The landing gear scudded onto the pavement and we shuddered to a halt before a dilapidated terminal. I emerged, with my fellow volunteers, into the cool mountain air and eagerly inhaled the scents of cedar and wildflower, wood smoke and ripened fruit.

Someone gestured to the edge of the runway and said, "They must have heard we were coming." Dozens of townspeople had gathered on the far side of the fence, their round faces peering through the chain links. Some waved, some tittered and pointed. Most just stared.

The women wore faded dresses with flowered prints and frayed hems, and they giggled into their knuckles with awkward timidity. Their cheeks looked swollen, wind-burnt, and their faces were lined with tribal tattoos, weaving patterns of solid and dotted lines assembled like mazes with no way out, their portentous angles and tapers simply fading into darkness.

The men watched with defiant determination, leaning forward on squat, powerful frames. Their arms and torsos were lined with tight, corded muscle, and they stared with unapologetically critical expressions. Over time, I would learn that Highlanders, by tradition, subjected everyone they encountered to the same scrutiny, assessing their size and strength, their potential as an ally or an enemy.

Shirtless children darted through the crowd, stopping for a moment to add their stares to those of the others before tiring of the inactivity and bolting again. They were coated in a layer of dust, which lightened the blackness of their bare chests.

The whole town seemed to have come to a halt to watch our arrival. We were twenty-five tall, lanky Westerners of delicate complexion, our skin burnt pink by our recent arrival. We stood, confused and nervous, as the Highlanders surveyed us with mouths ajar, hands clasped, one dusty bare foot kicked before the other.

The circus had arrived.

"You think they can tell we're not from around here?" someone joked.

"Oh, not you, Butler," another answered. "You've got 'local' written all over you."

We laughed and pulled our bags from a flatbed trailer towed behind a tractor, and an unobtrusive Highland man approached and introduced himself as Sonny, the Peace Corps driver. He would take us to our training center.

Several passengers climbed aboard the Land Cruiser, while Sonny secured their bags to the roof rack. The first group left, and I waited for the next transport. Others stood and chatted, watching the crowds watching them, but I wandered on my own.

I hadn't yet connected with the other volunteers. We all had certain things in common, dressed in old t-shirts and scuffed hiking boots. We were young, thin, unshaven, and almost all males – the Peace Corps had deemed Papua New Guinea unsafe for single women because of its high rate of violent crime, particularly incidents of sexual assault. The few women in our group were there with their husbands, while the rest of us faced the daunting prospect of two very lonesome years.

But the others came from a different world than mine, places like New York, Chicago, San Francisco– cosmopolitan centers everyone knew about. Most had traveled and even lived overseas, and they wore an urbane expression of comfort, even boredom, with this place, while I could only stare in wide-eyed amazement. In Moresby, everyone had spoken at length about why they joined the Peace Corps, but to me they just looked like they belonged. They were straight out of central casting, looking as if they had been destined all their lives to come to this very place.

I didn't feel that way. I felt like a fraud.

I wanted to calm my churning insides, to *feel* the way they looked. I wanted a purpose, and I thought I could find it by volunteering to help people whose only "fault" was the misfortune of being born poor. I wanted to create a sense of fulfillment.

I wanted to help; I just didn't know how. I knew there were flaws in the fabric of society and nature that caused poverty, but I didn't really understand what those problems were. I didn't know what it meant to be poor, or hungry, or to truly go without. Maybe in this place, I would learn. And maybe I would stumble upon genuine virtue, even if only by coincidence. But I didn't know how to express the uncertainties of what brought me here, so I kept them to myself. And I retreated into this feeling that I didn't belong.

When Sonny returned, we loaded up for another trip, and I climbed into the front seat. We departed, and the town of Goroka sped past in a blur of greens. People on the street hailed us as we passed, and Sonny returned their waves, a grin nearly obscured beneath the thick beard that hung from his chin to his breastbone.

"They all know you?" I asked, and he nodded.

"Do you come from around here?" I continued, and he nodded again. Still, he didn't speak, and I had surrendered to the silence when he drew a deep breath.

"My village," he said with a heavy accent, barely above a whisper, "is there." He gestured toward the deepening valley west of us, and then he turned and pointed to me. "This is the village where you will stay. Good people," he assured me, seeming to extract each word as if it had been trapped in the back of his throat, afraid to venture further. "They will take care of you," he avowed. I only nodded.

I knew our training coordinators had already chosen the villages in which the volunteers would be staying. They had already paired volunteers with host families, based on their assessments of us during those first days in Moresby. I wondered what they had seen in me, how they had made their decision. I wondered if they could tell how unsure I was.

It only took a few minutes to arrive at a gravel driveway, set back from the main road, where Sonny turned. This was the Catholic mission station called Kefamo, and over the coming months, it would be the site of our teacher training, as well as lessons on the language, history and culture of the Highlands.

If our experience in Moresby helped us physically adapt to this country, our time in Goroka would acclimate us culturally and teach us the way of life of the people there. Throughout our training, we would spend most of our time in the villages, working the gardens, eating meals and practicing speaking with our host families. Mornings, we would make our way here to Kefamo to talk about our observations. Here, we would formally study the language and take time to relax and write letters home.

Sonny stopped the Land Cruiser at a line of shady breadfruits and knotweeds that ran along a neat row of clapboard buildings. Two sets of bungalows were situated in parallel lines, separated by a cement pathway beneath a corrugated tin awning. The dwellings sat amid a lawn of sprawling, lush grass. Small ponds, fringed with sedges and orchids in bloom, dotted the expanse.

We were to spend one night here, before moving to our villages. It would be our last opportunity to take a hot shower and sleep in a bed. The next day, we would be delivered, one by one, to our villages and host families.

The room assigned to me for that last night was almost impeccably clean– a significant accomplishment in the South Pacific, where heat and humidity breed mold, decay and endless insect life. The smooth, painted cement floor gleamed in the light of the setting sun, without betraying a speck of dust. The bungalows were normally reserved for missionaries, so the walls were adorned with crucifixes and rosaries, which gave the room a feel of ascetic purity. With its Christian icons, the scent of chemical cleanser over whiffs of candle wax and aged wood, it could have been my grandparents' house.

And just like my grandparents' house, a painting of Jesus hung above the bed, his hands clasped before him in pained and compassionate prayer. I'd seen the image a thousand times, but it no longer meant to me what it once did – Catholicism was another piece of my childhood I'd left behind. But the guilt I found to be inherent in my erstwhile religion had followed me here, and I couldn't help feeling the painting was watching me, seeing through me, evaluating and dissecting me, just like the Highlanders watching us as we got off the plane.

I kept the window louvers open as I crawled over the thin mattress on its bare wood frame and turned my back to the painting on the wall. A gecko scampered across the ceiling, pausing for a moment to tilt his head and scrutinize me. A faint chill laced the air, and I pulled the threadbare blanket over my shoulders.

I tried that night to envision the villagers with whom I would soon be living, but their faces were elusive shapes without form or personality, like the landscape of the Highlands, concealing itself beneath the canopy. Images floated motionless before my eyes, which finally closed, no longer able to resist the burden of their own weight.

November 28, 1994 – Spirits

In Port Moresby, we had spent our first ten days living in the dormitory of a teachers' college on the outskirts of town. The bunkhouse buzzed with gnats, flies and mosquitoes, and anything we wanted to protect from the cockroaches had to be suspended from a laundry line that ran the length of each room. Even then, a determined line of ants conducted a nightly march down the wire to investigate and help themselves to what they could. Thus, I lost most of a bag of trail mix I had bought in the airport in San Francisco.

The sweltering temperatures and pounding sun in Moresby made for long days, and the evenings weren't much cooler. We were sore and feverish from inoculations against hepatitis and typhoid, and the side effects of our malaria preventatives included bouts of anxiety and vivid dreams. It all conspired with an unrelenting case of jetlag to wake me in the dead of each night, sweating, bewildered and unsettled.

The nearest bathroom was located outside the dorm, to mitigate its smell, and a green frog made its nighttime home in the decrepit toilet. I found him there at about 3:00 every morning, illuminated in a pool of jaundiced light that swarmed with gnats and moths. The frog clung, unmoving, to the curved inner wall of the rust-streaked commode, and he seemed somehow aware of the depths of my self-doubt. I sensed him mocking me from his perch, and I remember wondering if I'd ever sleep again.

But on the first night in the Highlands, I slept soundly, without interruption. I woke late the next morning and rolled slowly from bed, stretching limbs tightened by sleep, feeling hungrier than I had been in weeks.

I wandered down the path to a conference room with paneled walls and louvered windows, where a man with unruly gray hair stood staring at a wall-mounted map.

The island of New Guinea, of which Papua New Guinea occupies the eastern half, resembles a large bird perched above the tip of Australia's Cape York Peninsula. The western half of the island, a territory of Indonesia, forms the uplifted head and beak, while its midsection and tail taper downward to the east, forming the Papua New Guinean side. Two parallel chains of rugged mountains and dormant volcanoes, some reaching over 14,000 feet in elevation, are represented on the map by shaded relief sections, running along the spine of the island. A high plateau, crisscrossed and serried by steep valleys, conjoins the ranges. These are the Highlands, and it is here that most of Papua New Guinea's population resides.

The man pried his gaze away from the map and turned to me. He wore battered canvas sandals, dark shorts and a black windbreaker over a t-shirt reading "Oops– Wrong Planet." His weather-beaten Caucasian face sported creases around the eyes and mouth, and the flesh hung below his chin. Salt-and-pepper stubble textured his jaw, and a pair of tortoise-shell glasses perched at the end of his nose.

"Morning!" The eager tones of his American accent bounced to me across the empty room. "You are . ..?" I told him my name. "Yeah," he came over to me with a beaming smile, gripped my hand and pumped it vigorously. "I'm your training coordinator," he said. "Barry."

I glanced over his shoulder at the map and he followed my look. "What do you think?" he asked as his eyebrows peaked above his glasses. "Hell of a fuckin' place, isn't it?"

"I don't know." I shrugged, somewhat taken aback at hearing him drop an F-bomb at the beginning of our conversation, especially in the sterile confines of a Catholic mission station. "I just got here." And he laughed.

Barry stood six feet tall, with broad shoulders and sturdy legs. I guessed he was somewhere in his forties, only because his face looked a little older than the rest of him, but his eyes had a radiant gleam.

"You're an American?" I asked, and he nodded. "Where are you from?"

"I grew up in New Jersey." He pushed up his glasses. "But I've been in this country for ten years."

14

I pondered that for a moment. Ten years was exactly the length of time I had lived in Green Bay, and it felt to me like a lifetime. The exoticism of this country was undeniable – its beauty was spellbinding– but it was also riddled with poverty, crime, and corruption. Who could spend ten years here? Who would want to? I was daunted by the prospect of committing myself to two years here, and this guy had reeled off a decade like it was nothing.

"This is an incredible place," he said, as if reading my mind. "It doesn't let you go. Half the outsiders who come here don't ever want to leave. Plenty never do."

I thought back to the research I had done before coming here, the tales of explorers and adventurers who seemed to have been swallowed whole by this place. Two British missionaries, James Chalmers and Oliver Tompkins, went missing in 1901 at a place called Risk Point, off the south coast. No trace was ever found of them, but they were rumored to have been killed and eaten by a local tribe. Amelia Earhart, on her attempt to fly around the world, took off July 2, 1937 from an airfield in the town of Lae, less than 200 miles from Goroka, before she famously vanished. More than 2,000 Australian soldiers and thousands more from the Imperial Japanese Army went missing here during World War II and were never accounted for. In 1961, Michael Rockefeller, son of New York Governor Nelson Rockefeller and grandson of financier and philanthropist John D. Rockefeller Jr., overturned in his catamaran in the Asmat region of western New Guinea and was never seen again.

It seemed like this was a place people came to disappear.

"It's a spiritual place," Barry said, following the statement with a Papua New Guinean habit of saying, "ah?" It was part question, part declaration: a way of checking to see that you were keeping up with him. He tacked it so closely on to the end of the last word it became a part of the word itself. "A spiritual place-ah?"

He hastened to add, "But not in the way Westerners are used to that sort of thing," with a dismissive wave of his hand. "Spirits, ancestors, sorcerers. People here believe they're involved with even the simplest occurrences. Sickness, accidents, crops, weather, it's all controlled by the spirits. No one can avoid it."

15

When I think about it now, it seems uncanny that on the day I was preparing to move into my village, Barry talked to me about spirits. I should have asked him why it mattered. I should have asked what he was trying to tell me. How did their beliefs in the ethereal world affect the way they interacted with this one? What did it really mean to them? To me?

In the States, my family went to church every Sunday when I was a kid, but aside from that one interminable hour per week, it didn't mean anything to me. How was this different?

But I'd only just arrived. I wouldn't have known what to ask. Weeks would pass before the woman would follow us home to our village, and even then, I had no way of knowing what was about to happen.

I stared again at the map, its abstraction and uncertainty. "Have you ever had one of those dreams," Barry began, "where you're in the house you grew up in, and you find a door that leads to a room you never knew was there? It's been there all along, but somehow you didn't know about it. And you open the door and go into the room, and it's entirely different from what you expect, and yet there's something familiar about it that you can't quite put your finger on."

I sort of knew what he meant. I'd had those dreams, and I knew that sense of an alternative reality existing right beside me, bringing with it a maddening sensation that something important was before me, and it felt familiar because I almost knew it, almost had it, but some piece, infinitesimal but essential, wouldn't fall into place, leaving the rest to hover tantalizingly in the ether.

"Different cultures have different words for it. The French call it *presque vu*: the almost seen. In Welsh, they call it *hiraeth*: a longing for a place that doesn't exist." He gestured around us, grinning again. "Well, this is that place."

The lenses of his glasses magnified his pewter-colored eyes and spilled over his cheekbones. The glasses kept sliding to the tip of his nose, forcing him to raise his eyebrows and flare his nostrils to hold them in place, which pulled his upper lip over his teeth into a mischievous and perplexing grin. Combined with his puzzling depictions, Barry began to remind me of the Cheshire cat, and I was suddenly convinced that if the rest of him disappeared, that grin would remain. That, and maybe his smeared specs, which he pushed repeatedly back to the bridge of his nose.

I only half understood, but I nodded, salvaging some hope from the muddled enigma he described. Maybe this sense he was describing was the thing I had come here to find. Maybe I didn't have to generate the sense of purpose I sought. Maybe it was already here, somewhere, and I only had to find it.

I eventually found the dining hall, and along with the other volunteers I wolfed down a British-style breakfast of fried eggs, baked beans, toast and jam with tea. Afterward, we piled onto the open flatbed of a snub-faced Toyota Dyna truck, and Sonny drove us to town to purchase supplies from an arcaded row of shops near the airport. As we leapt from the truck bed, we clearly made a spectacle similar to our arrival the day before, for once again a crowd assembled to watch, standing shoulder to shoulder, staring as we filed past.

At the entrance to the shop, a drowsy security guard sat on a stool, a sawed-off shotgun across his lap and a boom box at his feet playing Haddaway's *What is Love?* at ear-splitting volume. The song had been a favorite in the clubs during my last year at college, and hearing it now reminded me of going bar-hopping with my roommates, watching the girls dance and laugh, hoping to make eye contact, egging and goading each other to go up and talk to one of them, trying to find bravado in beer and cigarettes.

Just a few months and 10,000 miles ago.

The interior of the shop sat draped in dust. Two aisles displayed canned and dried goods, sacks of rice and flour, Chinese-made pots and pans and basic needs in random arrangements. In one aisle, thong sandals and scattered undergarments sat in a haphazard pile along a shelf. Immediately below them sat several raw pine coffins, in a full range of sizes, from adult all they way down to infant.

I focused for a moment on the tiny casket, absorbing its mute statement. Babies die here. In fact, they die so often that the accessories for their disposal are sold alongside rubber sandals and tinned fish, as if they all existed within the plane of reality. I couldn't understand what perverse formula made that possible, and I turned away. I wanted to focus on beginnings, not endings, and certainly not on endings that never began.

I looked at the list of items we were encouraged to bring to our villages. Courtesy dictated that a visitor bring gifts for his hosts, so I would buy a few pounds of rice, some cans of chopped fish and braised meat, sugar, tea, cookies, a kerosene lantern, a machete, a water bucket. The tools of subsistence in the Highland villages.

I squeezed through the crowds and pulled goods from shelves, wiping away the dust to distinguish one item from the next. Most of the labels were in Chinese, with only a cartoonish picture of a leaping fish, a happy duck, or a winsome cow to suggest their contents. It was all so unfamiliar, there could have been anything in them.

I made some arbitrary choices and paid the cashier a few *kina* notes—multi-colored bills sporting images of crocodiles and birds of paradise. I emerged from the musky air of the trade store and into the soft mountain breeze to find Barry leaning against the truck, chuckling. The store had no frontage, just an opening like a garage, offering an unimpeded view of the shoppers, as if on stage.

"Why're you laughing?" I asked, as I loaded my purchases onto the truck bed.

He pushed up his glasses and tipped his chin at the other volunteers bumbling around the trade store, searching in vain for a lantern with unchipped glass or an undented can of fish. They were slowed to near immobility by the uncertainty of what they were doing, and the crowds jammed around them.

Barry just grinned. "It's amazing how far you guys'll come in the next couple of months, ah? It's fun to watch the light come on."

Barry waited with patience and humor. He polished his glasses on his shirt as the volunteers stumbled through the trade store, exhausted by the simple experience of grocery shopping. He hiked his sleeves over his shoulders, only to have them fall back down his arms. Restless, in need of activity, he fidgeted, busied himself as he waited.

A barefoot, bare-chested kid, with a round belly that he thrust proudly before him and a line of mucus descending from each nostril, strolled past us, rolling a muddy ball at the end of a forked stick. Barry hiked his thumb at the kid and said, "That's his car," as the boy turned a corner and was gone.

I wondered how someone like Barry ended up here, with no desire to leave. Outsiders in Papua New Guinea tend to fall into one of what Barry had referred to as "the three M's" – missionaries, mercenaries, or misfits. An Australian account of Papua New Guinea's colonial era, called *Taim Bilong Masta,* refers more bluntly to "the three Fs: fools, freaks and failures." They wander the country to make their homes in its rainforests, seeking fortunes to reap, souls to save, or a sense of belonging that eludes them elsewhere.

But Barry didn't seem to fit into any of these categories. He was the closest thing I had seen to those Peace Corps ads portraying volunteers with an implicit look of satisfaction. He had found his purpose. He had no doubt that he was in a place where he belonged and made a difference. And his certainty only made me feel less like I did.

As we organized our things and prepared for the trip to our villages, I wondered how I could develop a sense of fitting into this place. I tried to ignore the twinges of uncertainty and doubt that nagged at me. We departed and headed north, into the shadows of the high ridges.

We made our way out of Goroka along what is charitably known as the "Highlands Highway," a two-lane track that stretches westward from the coastal town of Lae, where Amelia Earhart was last seen, through the heart of the Highlands before petering out as a dirt trail just 100 miles from the Indonesian border. In Goroka, the road was asphalted with what the Australians call "bitumen," and its surface provided a smooth ride, allowing us to focus on our surroundings as we made our way into the valley.

Araucarias and fig trees, strewn with banyans and ficus, emerged from primordial clay mud. Vines, lianas and walls of bamboo overhung the grasses and creepers that sprung from hillocks. It seemed inconceivable that so much life could be packed into such a small space, all of it vying for every inch of light and air it could get. I could see how someone could find the jungle so claustrophobic as to be incapacitating, and yet the slopes were interspersed with clusters of bush huts and roundhouses, dwellings where people lived.

Narrow trails lined with elephant grass, sago palms and withered banana trees twisted their way from the road to disappear into the bush,

We turned off the road beside a ramshackle trade store with faded, peeling paint. A torn advertisement for Mutrus cigarettes flapped in the breeze, and a rusted metal chimney jutted from the roof, emitting a meager wisp of smoke. The door hung ajar, but the store sat empty; just a few bare, withered shelves.

We were on a dirt path now, and our ascent slowed amid the mud and scrub, as the trail was barely wide enough to accommodate us. Enormous potholes marred the surface, and we jostled about like insects in a collection jar.

Through spots of cleared foliage, we caught glimpses of the landscape we had overflown the day before. Forested mountains cloaked in mist ringed the ridges on all sides. Streams meandered along the valley, dappled sunlight glinting from tumbling waters. Narrow clay paths cut persistently through the bush to switch back and forth along the hillsides. The tapers and steep angles of the countryside made it feel as if the earth itself were sliding sideways into oblivion.

We stopped periodically to deliver the other volunteers to their villages, and their host families emerged to greet them. I watched with a strange sense of detachment, unable to envision my arrival or quell my anxiety. I was overwhelmed by the wooded chasm of the valley and the density of the forest, the hazards of the trail and the exoticism of the tiny villages, dwarfed by the towering wilderness.

Soon, I was the only passenger left, and as Sonny negotiated the trail, I practiced the few local phrases we had learned in our language classes. *Nem bilong mi…–* "My name is…"*Mi hamamas long bungim yu–* "I am happy to meet you." I mumbled them to myself.

We came to a ravine, carved by a stream that wound through the reeds fifty feet below. It was spanned by a decrepit bridge, two tree trunks felled alongside one another, a bunch of weathered slats nailed across them, reinforced by assortments of metal and iron beams. The planks didn't nestle together but overlapped at some points and left gaps at others. Many were loose or had fallen into the stream.

As we eased across, the logs sagged and creaked, and I felt a dizzying sense of spatial distortion, as if we were barely moving forward at all and each shift and shudder of the bridge were magnified ten times. I noted with trepidation that in the streambed below us lay the twisted, pummeled wreckage of a van. Its battered carcass lay on one side, the stream entering the engine block and exiting the rear hatch. Heat, rain and time had rusted away the chassis, leaving a half-submerged shell. Vegetation sprouted around the frame, embracing and engulfing it. Moss covered its sides, and grass grew through the frames of the windows and doors.

It must have taken years for the van to decay, as its bolts rusted, its metal skin oxidized and withered beneath the endless current, its seat cushions deteriorated, tires deflated and degraded, and the reeds grasped the meager light that pierced the empty gaps. But the pitiful carcass, now swallowed almost entirely by the forest, demonstrated in its own elegant way that the primacy of nature lies in its abundance of time. Nature has all the time in the world.

November 28, 1994 – Arrival

The village of Mari-eka sat just off the mountain trail, a few miles from the Highlands Highway. I don't even know if it's still there today – whole villages tend to pull stakes and relocate on a regular basis, seeking better land for gardens or grazing, or drifting with changing tribal boundaries and alliances. In those days, a curtain of ferns and creepers grew over a split rail gate, protecting the approach to the village, and we could easily have passed it without ever knowing. But this was the home of Sonny's people, and he knew where he was going. After crossing the bridge, he turned off the trail near the gate and halted in several inches of red clay mud. The clouded skies, droning insects and smells of wet soil and bitter wood smoke hinted something mysterious, almost ominous, lay hidden beyond the gate.

I thanked Sonny and shook his hand, and then I hoisted my duffel bag over my shoulder and descended the trail. The path was dotted with pig droppings, and rain had left the surface slick and muddy, so I took deliberate steps, worried that slipping into a pile of pig shit would have made for an ignominious arrival. I climbed to the upper rail of the gate and paused there, steadying myself.

Within the village, a cluster of fifteen roundhouses sat along the perimeter of a flat, treeless expanse of hard-packed clay. Several dozen people stood in the center. From atop the beam, I took my first look at my host family, and they at me. Sensing the significance of that instant, the importance of our first sight of one another, I smiled.

Overhead, finches and ploughbills whistled and screeched in frenetic tones that tore at the silence. The villagers and I watched each other, no one moving or speaking. Then, I jumped to the ground, and the crowd began to murmur.

A wailing call came from a voice hidden within the crowd. Others joined, and the sounds melded to form a steady, controlled wall of sound. Several elderly women, their sparse hair gray and their brown skin furrowed and desiccated, emerged with eyes downcast. They began to dance, flinging their hands at their sides as their bare feet slapped at the clay. The intensity of their cries and the rhythm of their dancing created an odd sense of euphoria. The villagers surged toward me, and the chants grew louder, more penetrating, almost deafening. Their tattooed faces made them look haunted, anguished.

A child ran his hand across my arm and then held up his fingers to see if the whiteness of my skin had rubbed off. Others moved forward, and suddenly dozens of hands began running over my face, shoulders and chest. An old woman embraced my legs as others pulled at my shirt or clutched my hair. Unseen hands pushed and pulled, causing me to sway with the surges of the crowd. My smile faltered. The sound pressed further, the hands and faces advanced closer, and a wave of vertigo washed over me.

Suddenly, a voice bellowed, and everyone stopped backed away from me to reveal a solid man with a thick beard. I guessed his age to be mid-thirties, though he may have been younger. It was impossible to tell in the Highlands, where the harsh elements quickly and prematurely age the inhabitants.

He stood with arms crossed, a stalk of grass clenched tightly in his teeth. He was at least a foot shorter than my six feet, but he was built of solid muscle, like a coiled spring, a bolt of energy. His plain work shirt matched the well-worn pair of old wool trousers that tapered to a frayed cuff at the middle of his calf. His stood with callused, splayed bare feet anchored in the thick mud. Raising his eyes to mine, his expression went from ferocity to delight.

He placed his fist against his chest and said, "*Mi papa bilong yu.*" My host father.

I told him my name, but he shook his head.

"*Nogat,*" he said. "*Nem bilong yu, Nipi'e.*" "Your name is Nipi'e."

Like that, I was rechristened the tribal name for a rare species of bird of paradise. And as quickly as it happened, I nodded in acquiescence. If I was to be their adopted son, it made sense that they should name me. I was giving myself to the people of this village, acknowledging their familial authority. I embraced the change of my name, because I thought it meant that all I had brought here with me, the disappointments of my past and the vagueness of my intent, might be left further behind. I was in their hands. I trusted them because I felt an instinctive sense that I could.

Besides, I really didn't have any choice.

Mari-eka sat at the edge of a bluff that gave way to a view of the valley below and the sea of green-gray mountains that flowed like a flood tide from the horizon. The stream that forged the ravine in front of the village also curled behind it, carving the plateau into an isthmus in the midst of the valley. Thick foliage clung even to the steepest slopes like a blanket, folded with lush green.

The clearing at the village center was called the *singsing* ground, where meetings, celebrations and ceremonies took place. My host father led me across the *singsing* ground to one of the roundhouses, and he opened the door to reveal a thin woman holding a baby. She smiled, and the skin of her face stretched taught across swollen cheekbones, adding hard years to her appearance. She wore a threadbare sweater with a dusty denim skirt that hung to her ankles. She grasped the child's chin between her finger and thumb and turned his face toward me. His eyes shimmered, then he screamed and buried his head into his mother's chest. I was likely the first white man he had ever seen.

The woman held her hand to her sunken chest and said, "Mama."

"Mama," I repeated. "*Mi hamamas long bungim yu,*" knowing how ridiculous it sounded. "Hello, Mother, I'm happy to meet you."

She gestured toward the baby. "Gilbert," she said, and he quieted at the sound of her voice. "*Brata bilong yu,*" her voice barely a whisper, billowing through her broad smile. "Your brother."

So, there we stood, this new and awkward family, smiling at one another, Mama calming Gilbert, none of us certain what to say. Papa took my duffel bag and beckoned me into the roundhouse.

I ducked beneath the doorframe and walked across the hard clay floor. A shelf of raw wood ran along the wall, and on it sat a tarnished metal pot and an iron frying pan. A shovel leaned against the doorframe, a couple of machetes beside it. The scents of mildewed earth, cooked vegetables and charred wood drifted from an open fire pit at the center. To the rear, an elevated platform of thatched bamboo was separated by a sheet hanging from the ceiling. On one side, a few blankets were spread on the floor. The other side was empty. My room.

In the States, I had grown up with a typical kid's bedroom: a twin bed and an unfinished pine desk covered in scale models of the very same fighter planes that had contested the air above these islands fifty years before. My dresser drawers perpetually hung ajar, clothes hanging from them like a child chewing his food openmouthed. An old stereo perched atop the dresser, loaded with punk and heavy metal albums. Music posters covered the walls.

Here in the Highlands, in my new home, my room would be a few square feet of bamboo matting, separated by a hanging bed sheet. I was moved by the meticulous arrangements they'd made for me, giving me as much space to myself as the rest of the family had, combined. I didn't have the words to express my gratitude, and a familiar anxiety surfaced in me.

I don't deserve their kindness. What will they do when they realize this?

Papa lowered my things along the wall, and I handed the food to him. "*Mi bin kisim dispela kai kai long famili bilong mi,*" I said, having rehearsed it many times. "I brought this food for my family." My voice felt small, timid.

He nodded and set the bag aside, then gestured grandly around the inside of the hut, "*Ol dispela,*" he said, "*bilong yu.*" – "All of this is yours." He gestured to Mama and Gilbert, "And we are your family."

I could only repeat the same phrase. "*Mi hamamas.*" "I am happy," because I didn't know what else to say.

We had been studying Melanesian Pidgin, or *Tok Pisin*, since our arrival in Moresby. It was a nonnative dialect that developed when the colonials first began settling New Guinea. The settlers brought local tribes into contact with one another, often for the first time, to work on copra and sugar plantations, and islanders developed a shorthand way of communicating with one another.

The language had a singsong cadence and a mystifying lexicon. Thus far, my vocabulary was restricted to a disjointed collection of words like *kai kai*, 'eat,' *was was*, 'wash,' *kakaruk*, 'chicken' and *pukpuk*, 'crocodile.' We had learned to greet people by saying, *monin*, *apinun* and *gut nait*. The complexities of communication seemed beyond my grasp, but the language itself wasn't very difficult.

Pidgin makes few changes of verb tense, and it really has only two prepositions: *bilong*, which means "belonging to" or "of," and *long*, which means pretty much anything else, depending upon its context. Its articles are confined to *wanpela*, meaning "a" or "the" or "one," *sampela*, meaning "some," and *dispela*, meaning "this" or "that" or "these" or "those."

Despite its uncomplicated dialect, the Papua New Guineans never suffered from its simplicity. Their capacity for understanding seemed endless. Experience and necessity taught them subtleties of communication more intricate than most Westerners could imagine.

The people of my village were attentive listeners, and they understood more than words, they interpreted nonverbal clues; facial expressions, hand gestures and tone of voice. A different octave, an arched eyebrow or a lifted chin spoke volumes. I often struggled to find words when speaking Pidgin, only to find the villagers simply nodding their heads, having already gathered my meaning from everything other than the words themselves.

Given their innate ability to read people, I think now about the ambiguity and unease I brought with me to that village. I thought at the time I was hiding it from them, but I have come to believe they saw it as soon as they saw me, the moment I arrived. In retrospect, knowing this only emphasizes the acceptance and the generosity they showed me on that day and the ones that followed. It overwhelms me still.

Papa suggested a *wokabout*, an inherited word that came from the old colonials, who used it describe the nomadic habits of the Aboriginal Australians. It can mean any kind of trip, regardless of the destination. Pidgin had synonymous phrases like *spin tasol*, which means 'just spinning,' or "*i go raun raun*," just going around, reflecting an abiding cyclical philosophy that all journeys return to the place where they began.

Papa's brother Francis joined us. He was taller and heavier than Papa, with a dense, round belly. Like most Highland adult males, he wore a bristling beard that hung to his chest. The three of us crossed the village grounds and entered the forest, and others joined us along the way. Another villager introduced himself as Tim, a lanky teenager with a round face pulled in a permanent grin that made you feel like he knew something you didn't, his dazzling teeth shining brightly against his dark skin. Tim had studied a few years at a district elementary school and spoke a little English, so he helped translate for me.

As we walked, Papa pointed out ancestral lands and tribal boundaries and told me who lived where. He gestured in one direction and said in Pidgin, "Bad people live there, who like to fight." He assured me our village was peaceful and wanted nothing more than to farm and hunt to feed their families. Sometimes, he conceded, his people were forced to defend their land, or their pigs or women, but he insisted it was never their fault. The other tribes, he said, were always the ones who started trouble.

He took care to call out and greet the local farmers as we edged their gardens, and not just as a matter of common courtesy. If a visitor didn't announce that his intentions were benign, the landowner might assume otherwise. A misunderstanding could quickly become a war. It had happened many times before. So, we observed the expectations of the culture, and everyone we met was interested, eager and polite. They shook my hand, marveled at my height, stared at my pale skin and blue eyes.

We rarely stayed long in one place. Papa had too much to show me, too many people for me to meet. Faces came and went; I couldn't keep track of them all. Most lived in or near Mari-eka and were relatives of my host family – people I would see every day.

One person now stands out from our *wokabout* that day. She came along the trail carrying a string bag filled with yams. She was probably eighteen inches shorter than me, with a gaunt, tired physique and thin ankles and wrists, which gave her a certain lilting grace, a delicate fragility, as if she were constantly struggling to steady herself. She wore a *meri* blouse– an oversized, formless shirt handmade of rough-hewn, colorful fabric with floral patterns– and a frayed skirt, and she smiled as she shook my hand. I remember the feel of the calluses on her fingers and palm, like coarse sandpaper.

She was probably in her mid-forties, though with her, too, it was impossible to tell. Her caramel skin and thinning hair were lighter-colored than that of most Highland women, and her forehead was rounder, overshadowing the small features of her face; the deep folds of her eyes, her sharp nose and sloping upper lip.

I would see her again a few days later, and again after that when she accompanied us on our walk home from the wedding of Mama's cousin, but even then, Papa had to remind me who she was. He must have told me her name on that first day, but it didn't stay with me. I wish now I'd made note of it, if only to place a more definitive marker to her. I owe her that. But if I ever knew her name, I have long since forgotten.

After exchanging a few pleasantries, she turned and went on her way that afternoon, her ankles wavering beneath her burden. I doubt I even watched her go.

What should become of the things we remember?

We continued our hike over ridges and valleys and eventually, we rested on a hill overlooking a field of sweet potato mounds. We spoke in short, enunciated sentences, smiling and nodding politely. The sun began to set, shadows lengthening across the jagged ranges, darkness creeping along the valley floor. A layer of cloud diffused the sunlight to a dull, somnolent orange, and a cool breeze waded through the woods as we watched the daylight slip behind the limbs and branches, falling toward the distant ridges.

I suddenly noticed a chafing and stinging in my forearms, and I held them up to find them inexplicably crisscrossed with tiny, angry, bleeding slashes.

Papa made a *tsk* sound and said, "*Kunai.*"

Kunai, known scientifically as *imperata cylindrica*, is also referred to as razor grass or sword grass. The shoulder-high stalks covered much of the Highlands, growing unabated and almost impenetrable in dense clusters of flat, rigid blades about an inch wide, often six or seven feet high. Its edges are razor sharp and slightly serrated, embedded with miniscule silica crystals that slice easily into the exposed skin of anyone who passes by and happens to so much as brush along the stalks. I hadn't even noticed the cuts on my arms as they were happening. It wasn't until sweat began seeping into the gashes, stinging like dozens of paper cuts, that I examined my arms and wondered where the blood had come from.

We sat amid a cluster of banana trees while overhead an airliner cruised on its way to Manila or Singapore, its condensation trail slowly dissolving into pale blue. I told them I'd come here on an airplane like that one, and they asked how big it was, how fast it went, how far it could go. I could only answer a few words in Pidgin, while Tim translated the rest, and the villagers furrowed their brows and looked at me with skepticism. For a while, we sat back and watched the jet creep across the stratosphere.

Part of me instinctively yearned to be on that plane as we measured the ease of its progress. Ever since I was a kid, my most common dreams were of flying, especially when I felt anxious or out of place. Wherever I was, some part of me always wanted to be somewhere else.

I knew that in my time here I would struggle, with the elements and with myself, as I fumbled with the rainforest and tried to measure the villagers' reaction to me. I didn't know these people, couldn't envision what they anticipated from me, yet I sensed them watching, waiting for me to do something. I felt the weight of their expectations, and watching that airplane, envisioning the anonymity of its passengers, I envied them. I wondered if they were looking down on this mountain from 20,000 feet, and I wondered what they in their imaginations made of it.

After a while, Papa stood. "It will be night soon," he announced. "It's time for us to leave." The tone of his voice left no room to argue.

Nighttime, Tim explained, was the time of the *masalai*, the spirits. At home in the village, we were safe from them, but at night, away from the security of family and tribe, we were all vulnerable.

Like my conversation that morning with Barry, I would come to regret not taking more notice of what was happening around me. Already, the villagers were revealing the extent to which their spiritual beliefs affected their way of life. It just didn't occur to me that this influence could extend beyond a simple fear of the dark, or a healthy respect for the unknown.

I have never believed in magic or mysticism, and I had long since left behind the religion of my upbringing. I have always believed that what exists in the real world is infinitely more powerful than anything formed in our imaginations. Seeing how my adoptive family adhered to their beliefs seemed innocuous to me, even charming. They respected and feared a power greater than their own. It seemed appropriate to the immensity of these rainforests, and I admired the depths and the certainty of their faith.

But what I would learn, what everyone seemed to be trying to tell me, was that the Highlanders' accommodation to the supernatural was more than a simple adherence to the tenets of folklore and mythology. Their belief in the spirit world was an intrinsic element of their very existence. They couldn't separate it from any other part of their lives. There was little distinction, a blurred and dangerous line, between the real world and the ethereal one. Crucial time would pass before I came to truly understand what that meant.

We returned to the village, and Papa prepared dinner over the cooking fire, the light of its flames dancing across the hut. He cut scallions and capsicum with one hand, pressing the blade of his knife against the calluses of his thumb, the same look of comfortable assuredness on his face that my dad back home wore as he shuffled around his kitchen in pajamas and reading glasses, frying eggs and mixing flour and baking soda for biscuits.

Papa boiled rice and stirred a sauce of tomatoes and pumpkin greens. He opened a can of mackerel by placing it on the ground, bracing it between his bare feet, steadying the point of his blade on the lid and driving it through, then turning the can to cut away the lid. He squatted, chin on his knee, and poured the tinned fish into his sauce, and I made a mental note to purchase a can opener for my family.

Tim and Francis were still with us, and another villager arrived, an ancient-looking man with bowed, spindly legs and a back stooped like a lobster's tail. Thin, withered flesh drooped from his skull. His ears had once been pierced, but the piercings had long ago been torn, and the bifurcated lobes now dangled in flaps above his shoulders. A skirt of *tanget* leaves modestly covered him, and aside from that, he wore only an old yellow sweatshirt. He had a natty gray beard, and a cigarette rolled in newspaper hung from his mouth, trailing rancid smoke. His dry lips parted to reveal a handful of scattered teeth.

He leaned on Papa's arm and cast a slow look, and when his gaze settled on me, he began nodding over and over. The flames of the cooking fire were reflected in the glistening of his eyes. I stood to shake his skeletal hand, and he spoke in a soft voice that wandered through the silence of the hut, whispering through the smoke. "*Mi hamamas,*" he said. "I am happy." He pointed to me with a finger that arched like his back, as if all the moisture had been wrung from his body, leaving a shriveled, curled husk.

Others offered their seats and helped the old man situate himself, treating him with the veneration reserved only for the aged, the respect to which a survivor is entitled. He sat gingerly at the edge of the hearth.

"*Kandre bilong mi,*" Papa told me, gesturing to the old man. "My uncle," he explained. "His name is Aha-no." I repeated the name and introduced myself as Nipi-e, and the old man smiled and nodded again.

Papa served the food, and everyone waited for me to start. I lifted some to my mouth and winced at the overly fishy taste of the mackerel. The flakes of meat were textured with scales and shards of bone, but I smiled at the others, who hunched over their meals.

Silence permeated the hut, interrupted by muffled compliments to the chef. Papa attacked his dinner with impressive appetite. I tried to keep pace, but he had given me more than I could finish. I ate all I could but soon conceded defeat. I patted my stomach and said, "*Pulap,*" "Full."

"*No,*" Mama jabbed an accusatory finger into my ribs. "*Yu bunating.*" "Nothing but bones." "Eat." Dejected, I returned the bowl to my lap.

After dinner, Papa squatted on his hams with his forearms on his knees and belched. "Nipi'e," he said. "*Nau em taim bilong stori.*" – "It's time to story."

It is tradition throughout the South Pacific that villagers sit beside the fires after a meal and talk late into the night. In Pidgin, they call it *stori*-ing. The conversations consist not so much of an exchange of ideas or opinions, or discussion of a consistent topic, but instead a loosely related string of stories. Themes are incidental, and the slightest element of one story can

31

lead to the next, the two having little in common. This was an intrinsic part of the oral tradition, the way the Highland people passed their history and their culture from one generation to the next. Barry told us one reason the villagers would be so eager for our arrival was that we would add new and different stories to their after-dinner traditions.

Papa *storied* about his impressions of me and my arrival in the village. A born showman, he made broad gestures, and his voice raised and lowered theatrically. At times, I heard him add "ah?" to the end of words, just as Barry had. Though I understood little, I sensed when he was being dramatic or humorous, and more than once I found myself laughing with the others at a joke I didn't understand, filled with the camaraderie of a shared experience.

Even so, I had never felt so conspicuously out of place. As helpless as a child, I viewed everything with absolute wonderment. It must have seemed funny to them then, as it does to me now. I was like a full-grown infant, unable to communicate or get by without someone to take care of me. They sympathized as they witnessed the awkwardness of what would amount to my second childhood, but they laughed at me in the same way they laughed at their own children.

Papa's brother Francis picked up where Papa had left off. He gestured to me repeatedly as he spoke, and everyone smiled or nodded. Francis lacked Papa's dramatic sensibility, but he had a genuine comedic flair, and everyone laughed long and hard at his story. Soon, someone else began, and the tales continued.

Evening faded to night, and I grew increasingly tired before the soporific fire as the stories floated across the smoky hut. The hazy illumination blurred, and my mind drifted, fatigued by endless phrases in a foreign tongue. I felt an odd familiarity with the words, but I was too tired to grasp them, put them together to assemble some meaning. I felt that sensation of *presque vue* Barry had described that morning –had I really just arrived at this place? I couldn't get it straight. My head hung forward, and my eyelids became heavy.

The old man, Aha-no, leaned toward me, and the hut fell into silence. He patted the crook of my elbow and spoke in the unique dialect of his tribe they called *tok ples*, which simply means "the language of this place." He pointed with a crooked finger toward my sleeping bag.

I shook his hand, marveling at his weather-beaten face, ashen despite the light of the fire. His smile gave an unselfconscious display of his few dark and decayed teeth, and he waved again toward my mosquito net. With some reluctance, I left the embrace of the fire and the storytellers, and I crept to the back of the hut to crawl inside my sleeping bag, as a rat scurried from the other side of the platform through a hole in the wall.

I didn't really sleep that night, but I didn't stay entirely awake, either. I lay on my back into the early morning, comforted by the silence and serenity of the dormant rainforest. I was unwilling to give up that tranquility, even in exchange for sleep, so I spent the night in semiconscious contemplation, watching dreams dance– my past and my future. As I stared at the dying embers of the cooking fire, long after the stories had vanished and everyone left, I wondered if it were possible for this to become routine for me, if I could ever grow so accustomed to the images of this strange, beautiful place that my senses could begin filtering them out, the way I grew to overlook the snow drifts and cow pastures back in Wisconsin.

But at that moment, I was too tired to try to answer that question, too tired even to sleep. Instead, I lay gazing into the encroaching darkness, on the far side of the world, the other side of anything I had ever known, and I waited for the sun to rise.

November 29, 1994 – Oases

In the pre-dawn darkness, I wiped a thin layer of dew from the face of my watch to find its hands pointing to a few minutes past five. Mama had started a fire, and its flames murmured and popped. Outside, a rooster let loose a hoarse, lonesome call that echoed and wandered through the hills. A metallic thrum filtered through the stillness as cicadas began to whine, while the songs of honeyeaters and swifts broke through the slight chill of daybreak, along with the shrieks of cockatoos.

Mama fixed a cup of black tea and handed me a couple of bananas and a yellow passion fruit. She didn't speak, but the silence between us nestled comfortably into the still mountain air. Crouched before the fire, I sipped from the mug and sucked the innards from the passion fruit, allowing the tart citrus to linger on my tongue and mingle with the vague bitterness of the black tea.

I looked forward to hiking the trail on my own, so I tried not to wake Papa. From across the fire, Mama watched me tie my boots, and when I finished, she handed me a *bilum*, patterned in blue, red, and yellow.

Bilums are shoulder bags, hand woven of string or plant fibers. Almost all Papua New Guineans use them, to carry anything from vegetables from the gardens to animals taken in a hunt, even their own children. They are an emblem of the Highlands, and of Papua New Guinea, in the variety of their uses, the complexity of their patterns and the varied brilliance of their colors.

"I made this for you," Mama said.

I stumbled through an inadequate expression of thanks, but she waved it off. She helped me tie the strap and loop the bag over my shoulder. She straightened the knot like a necktie and examined my outfit, ensuring my boots were properly tied, my raincoat easily accessible. She fussed over me like a mother sending her child to his first day of school. Then she released me, and I waved goodbye and ducked out the door.

The previous night had left the mountains immersed in mist, isolating the village, as if shielding it from the rest of the world. As morning fires heated the huts from within, the dew that had collected overnight evaporated from the roofs and drifted toward the gray sky in a gauzy haze. There was barely an utterance to be heard, aside from the cicadas and the occasional crow of a rooster or grunt of a pig, and these resonated dully against the tapestry of silence. A few people waved from their huts or called to me with soft, muted voices. The wet ground sucked at my boots and resounded with every step as the mud flowed back into the footprints it had left, pushing the air out with an eerie sigh.

I climbed the gate and approached the sagging bridge to find an ash-gray pig standing alone at the near edge, rooting through the *kunai*. He lifted his snout as I approached, seemingly resentful of my intrusion, and waited to see if I would find another way around him. We stood facing each other in a test of wills until I finally took a few steps forward and he abandoned his spot with an annoyed grunt.

Rocks and pits marred the way as I walked along the trail, and I tried to avoid the deepest pools of murky rainwater. I struggled to keep my footing on the slick surface, and slipped more than once. By the time I reached the main road, my shins and knees were covered in small scrapes and patches of mud.

At the Highlands Highway, I came upon a fellow volunteer named Dave, who stood wavering in the sunlight, looking asleep on his feet. Dave had a head of unruly brown hair, round glasses, and a long goatee, which covered a sheepish, slightly drunken-looking grin. He looked like a younger version of Colonel Sanders.

Dave came from Houston, the son of an engineer father and a psycho-therapist mother. The combination of his parental influences had given him an unceasing curiosity about the way things worked, especially people.

He said he had been a shy kid growing up, a good student who played the piano and the tuba. In high school, he spent a year in Sweden, where he came out of his shell and developed a desire to see the world.

He got a degree in economics and government from the University of Texas at Austin, graduating in three years, then took a job as a desktop publisher. He had once worked for what he described as a "shadowy entrepreneur," who sold Tbooklets on how to get rich on other people's money, and arranged franchises to connect clients with investment ideas and corporate headhunters. Naturally, Dave's boss charged a fee for introducing his clients, and eventually, he began helping himself to the escrow funds of the franchises he was supposed to be establishing. Around the time he started passing bad checks, Dave had the good sense to leave. Shortly afterward, the boss fled the office, leaving Dave's replacement in charge, mere moments before the police arrived to serve arrest warrants.

We all got a kick out of Dave's stories, told with understated humor in a slight Southern drawl that wandered in and out at random. We commented on the irony of the fact that he had come from a world of figurative headhunters all the way to this place, where literal ones reputedly still existed. His near miss with the law made him a mysterious, lonesome figure, a modern-day foreign legionnaire.

"G'mornin'," he said to me in a sleepy drawl.

I nodded and scraped dried mud from my elbow. "How was the first night in your village?" I asked.

He yawned, stretched, and managed to look bored. "Crowded, noisy, pig shit all over the place, nobody wears shoes. Kinda like back home. You?"

"Where I'm from, shit comes from cows," I said, "so I can't really compare."

Dave nodded, and a public motor vehicle, or 'PMV,' came along. Barreling headlong, it practically leapt a crest in the road, but as soon the driver saw us, he slammed on the brakes and skidded to a halt.

The PMV was a Toyota Hiace, a van with a blunt front end and an extended wheelbase. A wire grate was mounted over the windshield to protect it from rocks kicked up along the dirt roads. It had three rows of bench passenger seats, but it already carried at least fifteen people, plus a crying infant and what sounded like a small pig. The roof rack held *bilums* of *kau kau*, betel nut, mangoes, burlap sacks of coffee beans, and a cage holding several chickens.

It was a luxurious scarlet, a dense, arresting shade of synthetic candy apple red that clashed with the unrefined earth tones of the forest that framed it. I wondered what this van would have looked like when it rolled off its assembly line, when no one knew where it would be going. It would have radiated this crimson; lustrous and indelible, as if its manufactured vibrancy could somehow sustain itself against the elements, the way discarded polystyrene will linger for centuries before it succumbs to the will of nature.

But the PMV's appearance that morning demonstrated less of its prior brilliance than of the harsh realities of the Highlands. Rust and scratches robbed its gleam; dust and sunlight faded its hue, and dents so overwhelmed the chassis they fundamentally altered its shape. Only the tiniest hint of color remained hidden beneath the dirt, corrosion and scrapes.

This big red ball of misshapen metal on four bald tires ground to a halt before us. As the dust settled, the driver waved and smiled.

"Hello, America!" he shouted.

Dave and I approached the PMV with some apprehension. As a former British colony, the cars in Papua New Guinea follow the British style, with the driver on the left side, so as the PMV pulled up, the front passenger was nearest to us. He was a stout kid in a green rugby jersey with the number 37 on it and 'Winston Cigarettes' written on the sleeve. He hopped out and slid open the passenger door and Dave crawled inside. Then Number 37 climbed in behind him and gestured to me to take the front seat. I sat down and reached behind me to grab the seat belt, only to find there wasn't one. The driver shrugged.

"Okay!" he gave a thumbs-up, threw the column-mounted shift into gear, released the clutch and jammed his foot on the gas, fishtailing us into the road.

As we accelerated, the driver shoved a cassette tape into a stereo deck below the dash. An oncoming truck sounded its horn and sailed past us in a confused blur, and our driver hit his horn in return. The feeble sound of music playing at the wrong speed warbled from a speaker hanging by its wires at my feet.

The driver cursed and ejected the cassette, now trailing several feet of tape behind it. He handed it over his shoulder to Number 37, who began rewinding the spindle with his little finger.

I took the opportunity to tell the driver where to go: "*Mipela go long* Kefamo."

He laughed and nodded. "I know," he said, sticking with English, and added, "You speak Pidgin good." He took his eyes from the road and offered his hand. "My name is Joseph, and you are Americans with the Peace Corps," pronouncing it *Piss Corpse*. "You," he pointed at me, "are Nipi'e."

Before I could ask how he knew that, Number 37 had fixed the tape and returned it to the front. Joseph slid it back into the deck, and Steppenwolf's *Born to be Wild* blared from the speaker.

The van suddenly yanked from one lane to the other, and I turned to find a creature ambling off the bitumen surface into a ditch, unaware of how narrowly it had avoided a violent death. Joseph shouted, "Pig!" his accent making it sound like *peek*. He wagged his finger back and forth like a teacher scolding a student. "Never hit another man's peek. If you do," *tsk-tsk*, "you pay compensation."

"How much?" I asked as the trees whizzed through my peripheral vision.

Joseph tilted his head to the side. "Maybe," he paused and then yelled, "three thousand *kina*!" in triumph.

Three thousand *kina* equaled about US$2,000. He seemed to offer the number as an arbitrary sum, so I assumed he was making it up. I couldn't believe you would have to pay $2,000 for accidentally running over someone's *peek*, but I let out an appreciative whistle. Joseph whistled too and shook his head.

We hurtled along the road until we came upon another van, struggling at half our speed. Joseph maintained velocity and swerved, missing the van by mere inches.

"Jesus!" I exclaimed.

"Ah!" Joseph said, turning to me, "So, you are a Christian?"

Before I could get into a discussion over my misgivings about all organized religions, particularly Christianity, Number 37 leaned forward to ask, "Do you know Michael Jackson?"

"Who?" I asked.

Looking embarrassed, Number 37 leaned forward again, his head nodding with the bumps in the road. "Michael Jackson?" he repeated. "*Thriller?*" and I half-expected him to follow with "Seriously?" but instead Joseph reached back and nimbly smacked him in the forehead, and everyone laughed.

Eventually, the gravel drive and high fence of Kefamo beckoned before us, but Joseph continued at breakneck speed. I thought he might sail past it, so I made a halting gesture at the mission station, but at the last second, he locked the brakes, and we skidded to a stop. The contents on the roof shuffled against their restraints, including the poultry, which squawked in terror.

Number 37 popped open my door, and I dropped to the road on rubbery legs. I fished in my pocket for a few coins, but Joseph refused. "No, no," he said. "Free this time. Maybe next time? I will stop for you and we will ride together again."

"Ok," I agreed, certain that if I saw his van again, I'd dive into a ditch and hope like hell he hadn't seen me.

Dave dropped to the gravel roadside and we returned the waves of the other passengers. Joseph slammed his bare foot on the gas, and the van screeched onto the road, gone as instantly as it had appeared, and Dave and I gazed, dumbfounded, at the empty road behind him.

"Seemed like a good guy, didn't he?" Dave asked.

One by one, the other volunteers stumbled into the conference room. Our first night was behind us, and we told our tales quickly and loudly, each more interested in having his voice heard than in hearing the others. The din became deafening, and Barry sat at the front of the room, watching with mild interest, occasionally pushing up his glasses. He waited until the stories diminished to fragments before he finally spoke.

"Things are going to seem strange at first," he said, "but after a while, you'll find that what used to strike you as exceptional will become routine, ah? Remember, you're establishing a place for yourself in your villages." He paused for a moment. "Most of what you learn in this room will be basic speech, mannerisms, cultural norms. But as far as defining your role in this society," he pointed toward the mountains, "that happens out there."

He leaned back in his chair and was silent. Somebody said, "Some of the people in my village were calling me '*masta*.' Does that mean what it sounds like?"

"If you're asking if it derives from the word *master*, the answer is yes, it does," Barry said, and he shrugged. "That's what they were taught. And it's part of what I want to talk to you about today." He wheeled out an AV cart with an ancient television and a dusty VHS player, and told us we were about to watch film footage from the first expedition of Westerners into the Highlands, just sixty years before. Barry leaned his arm on the television and gave us some background, his inevitable grin firmly in place.

"For hundreds of years after the outside world discovered the island of New Guinea, the European settlers remained along the coast. They set up coconut and sugar plantations, mission churches and administrative outposts," he said. "They made a few forays inland, but they generally preferred the peace of the littoral plains rather than the mud and the mountains of the Highlands."

Legends abounded of mythical creatures residing among the steep precipices and dormant volcanoes. Evil spirits were said to cross the ethereal plain to sway among the trees. There was even a myth that one of the lost tribes exiled from the kingdom of Israel had ended its wandering among these mountains. The Europeans believed the center of New Guinea to be entirely uninhabitable, and for centuries, the Highlands were represented on maps with expansive blank spaces simply marked "unexplored."

In 1930, that isolation ended when a group of gold prospectors, led by Australians Mick, Dan and James Leahy, journeyed to a valley not far from where we were sitting. The prospectors expected to find a desolate landscape, devoid of life, in which to stake a claim, but instead they found a thriving region of over a million inhabitants, belonging to thousands of tribes, speaking hundreds of distinct languages.

The Leahys traveled with a motion picture camera, and in grainy, jumpy footage, they recorded the first contact between the Highlanders and the outside world. What they captured that day would become some of the most revealing and unique anthropological footage ever filmed.

"The Highlanders had never set eyes on a white man," Barry told us. "The day they met these Australians shook the foundation of their very existence. Until that day, they had been convinced there was no world beyond what was right in front of them. While the rest of the world believed there was no one in the Highlands, the Highlanders had believed there was no one else but them."

The footage showed the villagers fleeing into the bush at their first sight of the Leahy brothers, believing the white men to be ancestors, returning from the dead. They had no other explanation for their ghastly pale skin or their appearance from beyond the edge of the world. Other footage showed them retreating in terror as a piston engine airplane touches down in a field to resupply the expedition.

We watched them weep as they heard music coming from the speaker of a hand-cranked phonograph, believing the wooden box held the spirits of their deceased forebears, calling them from within. They swayed with the sounds and believed they danced with the dead. Their world had been turned upside down.

The Leahys failed in their quest to find gold in Goroka, but undeterred, they broke camp and headed deeper into the Highlands, leaving the villagers sobbing in lamentation of their abandonment by the spirits. Farther west, the expedition still couldn't locate the mother lode, but they found thousands more previously unknown inhabitants.

When word of this discovery reached the coast, a stream of adventurers and missionaries came plodding into the Highlands to stake claims of their own. A million people, who had never before heard of the Western god or the Christian Bible, had suddenly been discovered. The clergy raced up the mountains with the a fevered passion like the delirium that gripped the gold seekers. The Highlands were open for business, for prospectors and proselytizers, mining for gold and everlasting souls alike.

As more and more whites flooded the region, Australian administrators called "*kiaps*" began policing the Highlands through forest patrols. They kept peace among the tribes and enforced the rule of the colonials, protected the mission stations, trade outposts and independent fortune-seekers. The *kiaps* helped make permanent the presence of the outside world. First contact was over – the whites had come to stay.

Today, a determined expatriate community remains in Papua New Guinea, predominantly in larger towns like Moresby and Goroka. They come from Australia, China, the States, Britain, Japan and elsewhere. They teach in schools, run businesses, drill for oil or continue to seek the gold that drew the Leahys there decades before. They build schools and preach the word of their god.

After the video, Barry explained that to reinforce their authority, many of the prospectors, colonials and even missionaries would insist the Highlanders call them 'master.' The word *masta* became a part of the Pidgin vernacular.

"I don't want to reinforce that," someone remarked.

"I would hope not," Barry shrugged, "but people here don't much care about semantics. They learned a long time ago not to count on words. Chances were, whomever you were talking to didn't speak your language anyway. So, they learned to read people. Gestures, body language, attitude. That's what counts. They'll call you *masta* because it's something they recognize. You can ask them not to, and they'll respect that, but it won't change the way they think about you, because it was never a reflection of that to begin with." He looked around the room. "Words don't go far up here," he repeated. "What you do is what matters."

Following an afternoon studying Pidgin and dissecting the dilemma of inheriting the influence of the colonials, the day's sessions ended. It was time to return to our villages. We headed toward the gates with mixed feelings, reluctant to leave the clean floors and cushioned chairs. As I made my way along the cement path, two other volunteers, Brent and Dieter, walked in front of me.

Brent looked like a poster boy for the Peace Corps: tall and lean, with sandy hair and a narrow, angular face. He usually wore an intensely serious expression, as if grappling with a deep philosophical question. People seemed to perplex him. Their perspectives and their actions never seemed quite to match his. He wasn't the type to judge others based on their differences, but they always seemed to surprise him. And it was seldom the Papua New Guineans who baffled him; instead it was us, his fellow volunteers.

He was a quiet, agreeable guy, patient with the sarcasm and caustic humor of the others, though he seldom shared it. He was earnest and enthusiastic, and his zeal was infectious. Everybody liked Brent.

Dieter looked like he had just stepped out of a clothing store catalog. He could have been a wind-burned fraternity brother on a surf trip or a ski weekend. He had dirty blond hair and a baby face, marked by the Germanic features implied in his name. His clothes had a worn look but fit as if they were tailored specifically for him. He was confident and funny and gave the impression he would always land on his feet; the kind of guy everyone envied, but no one begrudged.

Dieter was born in Trinidad, Colorado, a former frontier town where Bat Masterson doled out pioneer justice a hundred years before. By the time Dieter was born, Trinidad had morphed into a hippie commune, whose inhabitants lived in harmony with the earth. His first pets, he told us, were goats and chickens he raised and cared for and then slaughtered as food for his family. He didn't have toys as a child, but never knew what he was missing, because none of his friends did, either.

His parents separated when he was young, and he spent his adolescence bouncing around the Midwest with his mother. He went to high school in Michigan, but came back to Colorado for college, maybe trying to capture the simplicity and certainty of the childhood he had spent there.

He joined a fraternity in college, and then spent a semester studying abroad. Like Dave and so many of the others in our group, his time overseas awakened his interest in the world around him. He had joined the Peace Corps when he graduated.

Dieter's host family called him *Lemokave*, the local name for the village gardens. He soon realized his new name was an anagram of "make love," which caused him to recount the amorous conquests of his college days. The stories only underscored the bleak romantic outlook we all faced, and we demanded he stop, but he persisted, and in some way, his tales helped us hold on to something of what we were missing.

"Hey," Dieter said to Brent and me as we walked along the path, "you know that hotel by the airport?" We nodded. "Did you know there's a bar there?"

* * *

The Bird of Paradise hotel sat just off the Highlands Highway, an airy mirage of marble floors, brass handrails and carved woodwork. The bar was in the back, where a terrace led to a well-kept lawn and a swimming pool, all of it fenced by a high wall. As Dieter, Brent and I arrived that afternoon, a few Westerners wallowed listlessly in the pool and a few more sat at the bar. A thin Papua New Guinean bartender in a dress shirt and *laplap* stood with his hands clasped behind his back.

"What kind of beer do you have?" Dieter asked him.

Before the bartender could respond, a voice answered in a heavy Australian accent, "They's only one kinda piss in this country. It's called SP, and I wouldn't feed it to my dog."

We turned to find a heavyset woman in a flowered dress, slumped against a plastic chair. The flesh hanging from her arms and neck was so pale it was almost translucent, except on her face, where heat rash tainted it an angry red. Her eyes were shaded beneath a wide-brimmed straw hat, from which sprouted frizzed tufts of strawberry hair. In one hand she held a fistful of damp, wadded napkins, and in the other, a paper fan. She had a look on her face of vague disgust, but she waved us over.

"Sit down," she said, pronouncing it *sedan*, and then she shouted, "Three stubbies!" She turned to us again. "My shout," she said. "I'm Shelly," and she offered us one hand while she brought the wadded napkins to her neck to dab at perspiration with the other.

"Thanks," began Dieter, "so, um, where are you from?"

"Sydney," she said with pride, then eyed us with evident doubt. "You're American, ain't ya?" We nodded. "How long ya been in country?"

"Two weeks," Brent said, and Shelly burst out laughing.

"I could tell," she said. "Ya blokes're green as hell."

Shelly, we learned, had been in Papua New Guinea for six years, which she pronounced *yees*. "Six yees in this fackin' place," she told us. "Tae bloody hot, else it's raining. Bloody food is shit…" she trailed off, mopping her skin again.

The bartender delivered our beers, and I took a drink from the short, stubby bottle. Despite Shelly's dismissals, the SP wasn't bad. It was a crisp lager, and it came ice cold. I took another pull as Shelly continued.

"Problem with these people is," she lectured, "they dan' want our help.

44

Got it pretty good up hee, and they dan' want anyone muckin' it up. We give 'em money, equipment, train 'em to use it, but we expect 'em to do samthin' with it, an' they dan' appreciate it. They take it for granted, git lazy. A genetic thing, I reckon." She leaned toward us conspiratorially. "They ain' too intelligent, see?" She pointed to her head. "Nah need ta be. Haven' gotta dae much to get by in this pat of the world. Food pretty much grows by itself, the land is all owned by the villages. Nah need to have a job. That's hae come the government is sa corrupt. Dan' think twice 'bout lyin' or stealin'. Ya can't trust any of 'em, not one bit." She held up a plump, pink finger.

She went on, and the three of us exchanged furtive glances. Shelly didn't share Barry's view of the magic of this country, yet she had been here almost as long as he had. That didn't make sense. Why would she stay?

Her diatribe confused us. We'd barely heard a word spoken against this place since our arrival, and we didn't want to hear one now. This was a struggling country, but it was a riveting land, and we wanted to believe we'd come someplace special.

Despite the distance from home and all I knew, or maybe because of it, Papua New Guinea seemed unspoiled, unsullied, practically perfect in its way. I had left behind the locus of my unhappiness, and I had arrived at the possibility of Eden, among others in whom I saw the dedication and passion for humanity I wanted to find in myself. While I questioned whether I deserved this opportunity, it offended me to hear someone intrude upon my notions of the purity of this country. I resented the implication that it was tainted. I didn't want her to disrupt the sense of euphoria I was trying to cultivate.

So, I shut her out. Her rant became a drone in the background, balancing on the fringe of my consciousness. Instead of listening to her, I watched the humidity condense on my bottle as the beer grew warm and flat. Out of politeness, I continued to drink, trying to wash away the bitterness that flowed from this strange woman.

"... white women ain't safe at all," she was saying. "Can't bloody leave tha house efta dark."

Dieter finally asked how she had ended up here.

45

"My husband works in construction," she explained. "Came on a two-yee contract."

"But you've been here six years," Brent pointed out.

"He extended," she said.

"Jesus!" I exclaimed more adamantly than I had intended. "If it's so bad here, why do you stay?"

"The money's bloody good," she answered.

"Seems like you'd be anxious to go," said Brent, peeling the label off his beer.

Shelly began to get agitated. "It ain' always that simple…" she began, and then her voice trailed off, as if she realized she was revealing more than she intended. There was an awkward silence.

Brent and Dieter and I managed to change the subject, talking about our villages and host families, and Shelly remained quiet for a while. She concentrated on squeezing lime wedges into her highball glass of gin and tonic. One by one, she squeezed them over the glass, then dropped the rinds into the drink. After several minutes of this, the glass was filled with rinds, leaving barely enough room for the drink. When she finally raised the glass to her lips, she found me staring.

"Wha's your problem, then?" she growled.

Awakened from my stupor, I shook my head. "Not a thing," I said, and hoisted my beer. "Cheers." Shelly and I tapped our drinks, and I downed my beer and stood.

"Well, ladies," I said, nodding at all three of them, "it's been a pleasure, but I gotta go." Dieter and Brent quickly latched onto my departure.

"Right, boys" Shelly said. "Piss off, nah. I'm sure we'll be runnin' into each other again. This ain' a big place."

"We'll keep an eye out," I promised, and we beat a retreat.

That night in the village, we ate another meal of rice with a stew of vegetables. Again, Papa gave me a huge portion, which I again failed to finish, subjecting me to the sting of Mama's scorn. The women left with the dishes while the men squatted on their hams to *stori*. More visitors came, including the old man, Aha-no.

They kept the conversation simple enough for me to follow if I concentrated, but after a while I grew too tired to try. I stared into the fire, nodding off, as they talked and laughed and told their tales, and I heard my name repeatedly. I smiled, but did little more to involve myself, instead merely watching and listening.

In their friendliness and their eagerness, in the warmth of their kinship, I found it impossible to reconcile these people with the thieves and brutes Shelly had described. She was a cynic, I told myself, a victim of her own pessimism, and it had rotted her from within. She hadn't left the outside world behind; she had brought it with her, and it didn't belong here. She didn't belong here. Maybe none of us did, but we at least sought some way to fit, some sort of purpose. Shelly, it seemed, had given up.

Later, after I had dozed off, a coarse hand shook my shoulder, and I awoke to find most of the others had left, and only Papa and Aha-no remained. The old man again smiled his gap-toothed smile and pointed to the back of the hut with his shuddering finger. I stood, and then turned to him.

"I'm sorry I didn't story much with my family, I'm just tired," I said. "*Na tok tok bilong mi em i nogut tru.*" "And I don't speak the language well."

The old man shook his head, the flaps of his ear lobes brushing over his bony shoulders. "*Bihain,*" he promised. "Later." "*Yumi gat planti taim.*" "We have lots of time."

I only wish that had been true.

November 30, 1994 – Photos

The scraping tones of whining cicadas filtered into the hut and grew increasingly loud and insistent. A dog growled and dug at the outside of the wall, while a voice from across the village laughed and then lapsed into silence, as if shamed by its own sound. A sheen of sweat covered me, and my sleeping bag chafed against my skin. I angled my watch to the kerosene lantern – it was 5:15. Rising to my feet, I heard a rustling on the other side of the partition, and Mama's hushed, sleepy voice called, "Nipi'e?"

"*Bai mi was was,*" I said. "I am going to wash."

My struggle with the language seemed more distinct in the silent darkness, while the calm hush of my host mother's voice only complemented the placid dawn.

"Wait," she whispered in Pidgin, "your Papa will go with you."

"It's okay," I protested. "I can go alone."

"No," she insisted, "you wait, and your Papa will go with you."

I knew solitude was a luxury rarely found among Highlanders. There was nothing to hide and nowhere to hide it. Their homes, their possessions, their lives, belonged as much to one another as to themselves. I couldn't ask to be an exception, so I waited.

Papa appeared, yawning and scratching his belly, and we left together. The sun had not yet risen, but pale blue streaks had begun creeping across the dark slate of eastern sky. It was enough to awake some thrushes, whose treetop whistling echoed across the stillness as my boots squished in the mud, the laces flapping haphazardly.

We climbed the gate and followed a path that veered away from the road before the bridge. The gray pig I'd seen the day before stood firm again among the hibiscus at the edge of the trail, and I decided to call him Wilbur, after the pig from *Charlotte's Web*, a book I loved as a kid. Wilbur again seemed dedicated to barring our way, but Papa gave him a swat with his bare foot, and he obviously sensed it would not be a good idea to tangle with Papa, so he lumbered into the bush with only mild irritation.

The soles of my boots were coated in mud, making for tough going as we eased down the incline. I lost my footing in the slick grass and was only kept from sliding into the ravine by Papa, who caught me by the arm and said, with mild understatement, "It's no good if you fall."

We came to the end of the path, where a small waterfall flowed into a brownish pool, where specks of sediment spun and swirled in the eddies. I pulled my shirt over my head and felt pinpricks of cool morning air against my skin. I kicked off my boots and shorts, while Papa watched with abstract interest.

The paleness of my skin and the sharpness of my features seemed to fascinate him in a clinical sense. He'd seen few white people in his life, and he'd never really known any of them. There was no judgment in his stare; it was acceptable and even expected in his culture, and I tried not to let it bother me. Stripped, I stepped across the muddy rocks and into the water.

"Papa?" I asked to overcome the awkwardness. "Tell me about Aha-no."

He sat for a moment, considering the question. "*Em i lapun,*" he said. "He's old."

"*Hamas krismas?*" I asked, "How many years?" as I plunged my head beneath the surface, the cold water sending a piercing jolt straight into my lungs, trapping my breath.

I emerged and exhaled to find Papa considering the question. Finally, he said, "*Lapun tumas*" which sounded unmistakably as if he were saying "Too old," but a mor accurate translation would be, "Very old."

I couldn't guess the old man's age. His face was grizzled, his chest sunken, and the muscles of his limbs looked atrophied. His flesh hung loose and unencumbered, like a child in a grown man's suit. His hands shook as he smoked ratty cigarettes rolled in newspaper, and he had a rasping, hacking cough.

"Tonight," said Papa with finality, "he'll sit and eat with us. We'll talk."

49

Papa suddenly paused and tilted his head. I stepped from beneath the waterfall and heard kids giggling. From a ledge at the top of the hill, a dozen little faces peered through the tall grass, pointing at me, and nudging each other.

"Bah!" Papa shouted to them. "Go!"

The peeping toms remained at their perch, so Papa scooped up a few stones and started throwing them at the kids with phenomenal accuracy. The rocks hummed through the air and whipped over the grass. One of the kids stood to run and a stone pelted him in his rump. He scampered up the hill clutching his butt, and the others howled with glee.

I retrieved my towel while Papa kept a watchful eye on the ledge. He held another stone, arm cocked, and I pulled on my clothes and assured him it was okay. The kids' curiosity didn't bother me, and I laughed as we made our way back up the trail.

The ride to Kefamo that morning was less eventful than that of the previous day. I caught another PMV, again filled to capacity, but this time the driver was deliberate and cautious. I sat in the back, among several politely curious passengers clutching *bilums* filled with crops, and a whining piglet tied to a length of twine scurried at our feet.

We dropped some passengers at an open-air market at the side of the road. Vendors sold *kau kau*, taro and sugar cane, as well as yellow, green, red, and purple bananas displayed on multicolored blankets and *bilums* spread across the mud. The sellers were mostly women, sitting side by side in *meri* blouses and long skirts, their bare feet crossed at the ankles, blunted toes fidgeting.

Among them, I recognized the broad forehead and butterscotch skin of the woman I had met on our *wokabout* two days earlier. She saw me too, and her thin mouth spread into a smile as she nodded to me. She gave a brief wave with a stiff hand, her fingers curled as if by cold, curving to practically clutch at her empty palm.

I remember sitting in the PMV that day, studying the women in that market and the familiarity they shared. The women of Mari-eka had the same ease, but their contentment would dissipate any time I interacted with them. There was a greater distance between me and the women, even Mama, than there was between me and the men, with whom I had already hiked and storied and was coming to feel at ease. I knew almost nothing about women in the Highlands – only that their lives consist mostly of labor and hardship.

Most children of the mountain tribes spend their first few years playing around the village and in the nearby woods, rarely straying far from home. Before long, childhood, especially for girls, is inevitably sacrificed on the altar of necessity. By around the age of five, they are expected to begin learning to tend gardens, clean clothes and dishes, and care for other children.

There is little opportunity for education, and girls are less of a priority than boys. If they are lucky, Highland girls might get a few years' elementary education at a district school, seated on the dirt floors of bush material class-rooms. Communities chip in to pay the fees of those few kids lucky enough to be admitted into district elementary and high schools, and those students are then burdened with the cumulative expectations of the entire village.

As adolescents, girls and boys may flirt, but they don't "date." Complicated cultural heritage, further convoluted by the influence of Christian mission-aries, has banished intimate relationships to the forests, where girls and boys explore and experiment away from the disapproving eyes of adults. It's easier that way, but it's also less safe. Statistics suggest as many as three quarters of all Papua New Guinean women are raped at some point in their lives. In the persistently and often brutally patriarchal society of the Highlands, the perpetrators are rarely punished.

It is common for girls to marry as teenagers, in a ceremonial exchange arranged by the families, who receive a negotiated bride price from the family of the groom. Mothers give birth to their children either in a dark hut or out in the bush. Physicians and medical facilities are rare, so births are usually unassisted. A midwife or an elder woman may tend to the mother, or she may go it alone.

Adult women are expected to gather water and firewood, cook meals, wash clothes, tend gardens and care for children. They sell excess crops in local markets and use the revenue to purchase basic necessities like rice or salt, a new machete or bucket.

Most of the women at the market that day looked to be in their mid-forties. They could reasonably have expected to live another ten to twenty years. Villagers make accommodation for their elders, but seldom more than is practical. Everyone lives in the same environment and deals with the same hardships; no one can be protected from the totality of the elements. The elderly continue to work, tending gardens, digging *kau kau* and hauling firewood, for as long as they are able, and they are sheltered for as long as they provide value. Once they can no longer contribute to the welfare of the village, it becomes less of a priority to safeguard their wellbeing.

As our PMV pulled away from the market, I again focused on the road before me, giving little more thought to the women who chatted amiably, laughed easily and halfheartedly tended their market stalls.

I must have returned the wave of the woman that morning, but I don't specifically recall doing so. The image I have of her now is overshadowed by what would happen to her in the coming weeks. In other circumstances, I doubt I would have given her another thought. Instead, I try now to reassemble her, reimagine her, so that I might know her today in a way I didn't then. All that I know of the women of the Highlands – wives, sisters, daughters, friends – I can only project onto her.

I don't know if I can reconstruct her now, years later, past the end of what would have been her natural life expectancy, so that I might somehow know who she was then. It seems farfetched, but maybe it's not so different from what I do with anyone else I knew during my time in Papua New Guinea– my host family, our trainers, the other volunteers, even myself. I put us all back together from fragments, impressions, wishes and memories.

What should become of the things we remember?

I stumbled into Kefamo half an hour late that morning. The others had gathered in the conference room to discuss Papua New Guineans' perceptions of Westerners.

"I just want to be treated like everyone else," Brent was saying.

"Yeah, but you're *not* like everyone else. This," Barry held up an arm to gesture at his white skin, "means you will always be viewed differently in this society." He stretched his shoulders, reached an arm behind his neck and snaked his hand over the top of his head to pull up his glasses; an awkward move that he somehow made work.

"When the whites first got here," he said, "they had native people do everything for them. They carried bags, dug wells, tended crops, served food, and cleaned the mess. It never occurred to the Papua New Guineans they were being taken advantage of. They figured the Westerners must be weak, otherwise they'd do the work for themselves, ah? If the 'white man's burden' was to civilize and evangelize the black man, then the black man's burden was to ensure that the white man didn't end up dying of exertion or any one of a thousand different deaths while doing it." He paused a moment. "That past is a legacy we all carry with us," he said. "You're lugging around a lot of history, whether you want to or not, and some of it's not very good." Now he grinned. "You guys who went to the bar yesterday probably saw some of what I'm talking about, ah? Behind the walls topped with broken glass and razor wire?"

Dieter and Brent and I exchanged sheepish looks, while Barry shook his head. "There's no law against going to the pub. But remember, there are no secrets in this place," he said cryptically.

We didn't bother to ask how Barry knew we'd been to the hotel bar. Instead, we told him about our conversation with Shelly, and he only nodded.

"Do you know her?" I asked.

"Nah," he said, "but I know the type. Can't stand it here, but can't seem to leave. Probably been here bitching about the place for ten years."

"Six," corrected Brent.

"So far," Barry added, "but she's not going anywhere."

I asked the same question I had posed to Shelly. "Why not? Why would she stay here if it makes her miserable?"

The smile crept back across Barry's face. "I told you, this place is different. Lots of people here claim to be miserable, and they talk constantly about going, but never do."

I shook my head, not really understanding that explanation, but I knew my frustration didn't come solely from Shelly. I was afraid of falling into the same trap she had. It seemed easy for her to sit at the patio bar, fanning herself, sipping gin and tonic, griping about her situation. She wasted no effort dispatching her warnings, her dismissals and her hatred. I even understood it. I understood the specific and virulent hatred of a personified place. I could relate to the blame and the pessimism she purged from herself and projected onto this country. I had done the same thing with place where I grew up. I knew my own susceptibility to that simplicity of thought, and I feared it.

But what I feared just as much was the possibility that she might be right. She'd been here six years; she knew this place better than I did. And if she was right, if our time and work here turned out to be futile, would I end up like her, angry and helpless? Sitting on a bar stool, unable to go home and face the world I'd left behind, telling newcomers not to bother with this place? Pulling them into the same cycle from idealism to disillusionment to jaded resentment?

"You'll see people like her everywhere you go in this country," Barry went on intruding on my thoughts. "Everybody's got a different story, a different reason for being here. Don't try and figure 'em out. And don't let them bring you down."

Climbing the trail that afternoon, I came upon a cluster of huts about half a mile from Mari-eka. A hut on stilts overlooked several roundhouses. Papa had told me a relative of his lived there with his three wives.

A man in a thick winter coat stood at the hearth of a charred fire pit. He was almost as tall as me, and his face was clean-shaven, both rare attributes for a Highland male. But rarer still was the ski jacket he wore. It was a beautiful day; in the low eighties with a gentle breeze, yet he stood there in this bright blue and scarlet coat, staring at the sky until he saw me and waved. I waved back and continued along the trail.

"Nip'ie!" he called to me.

The man approached and introduced himself, without a trace of irony, as Elvis. The ubiquity of American culture had pervaded even the recesses of the South Pacific. In my time there I would meet more than one Elvis, several Rambos, and a number of Michael Jordans. Shaking hands with Elvis, I tried not to picture him with lamb-chop sideburns and a glittery jumpsuit.

"I am your Papa's brother," he told me, though I didn't think that was technically true. I didn't remember how Papa had described him, but he hadn't said they were brothers. In fact, I remembered getting the sense he didn't like Elvis, saying he was primarily known for the brutality with which he beat his wives.

Domestic violence is sadly common in the Highlands, and during our training, many of the other volunteers witnessed it in their villages and within their host families. I never saw Papa lift a hand against his wife, but Elvis had evidently earned a reputation for the frequency and severity of his beatings.

He also was reputed to be a *raskol*, the Pidgin name for the criminal gangs that robbed buses and trucks along the Highlands Highway. At first, their crimes had mostly amounted to petty theft, but more recently they'd graduated to carjacking, rape and murder. Our trainers had cautioned us about them, but we laughed off the warnings: the name just didn't sound very menacing. My dad used to call our cat a rascal. The word evoked a mischievous child, not a dangerous criminal.

Elvis escorted me between three tiny huts toward a larger one, set back from the others. The smaller huts were roundhouses, like those in my village, but Elvis' hut was larger, and rectangular. It was luxurious by village standards, even ostentatious, a bush-material imitation of the prefab kit houses that clustered around Goroka. It sat elevated on wooden stilts, a few feet above the ground.

We passed a large fire pit, at the edge of which sat a metal pot with dented sides, blackened from open flame. The pot was half-full of days-old rice, dried and crusted to the sides. I must have turned my nose at the flies buzzing around the edges, and though I didn't say anything, Elvis saw my reaction. He cursed and kicked the pot with his bare foot, sending it tumbling into the fire pit in a cloud of ash, scattering the flies and flinging bits of dried rice.

I knew his response was a show for my benefit – this wouldn't have been the first time he had seen the pot. What he saw was my disapproval, and though it would have been slight, and unintentional, it wasn't lost on Elvis. I was struck by the power it held. I needed to be more careful.

Elvis stormed to one of the huts and pounded on a support beam, bellowing at someone inside. The door opened a crack, and a timid face peered out: a girl of fourteen or fifteen. Elvis pushed the door the rest of the way and the girl emerged, her face lowered, eyes fixed on the ground. She twisted past Elvis and then past me, and I berated myself for what I had started. She cowered and flinched, and I wondered if Elvis would hit her in front of me, and what I would do if he did.

She was only a kid, her face and neck still swollen with baby fat, and she was obviously terrified of him. She didn't dare look him in the eye as she slouched past. She grabbed the pot from the fire pit and ran back toward the dark interior of the hut. Elvis extended his hand to close the door, and she raised her arm reflexively before her face. He looked at me and shook his head in exasperation, as if I would commiserate on her laziness. I kept my face noncommittal.

Barry had already spoken to us about the omnipresence of domestic abuse in Papua New Guinea, as common in the public markets as it is in the privacy of the huts, if not more so. "This is a 30,000-year-old culture," he said. "You may have something to offer them in terms of living with modern technology or learning to speak the world's current lingua franca, but there are certain things that you may have to leave alone, and unfortunately, domestic violence is one of them."

Elvis and I walked on, without conversation, to the hut on stilts. He climbed a small bamboo stepladder that leaned against the doorway of the hut, and I followed.

"I will make tea," he offered, and I nodded.

As he put the kettle on the gas stove, he asked me, "You are happy in the village, with your family?"

"I am," I said, feeling anxious to leave. "They're waiting for me."

He shrugged off his jacket and nodded but began telling a story anyway. "Some years ago," he began in slow Pidgin, "a man came here, who knew about science. He was from France."

He said the man's name was Frank Magna, and he was an anthropologist. He had come to the Highlands to conduct research on traditional societies.

As Elvis spoke, I glanced around the hut at an odd assortment of items collected there. Most of them seemed out of place: a footlocker full of books and papers; a camera; hiking boots; a violin case leaned against a far wall amid scattered clothing.

My Pidgin wasn't sufficient to understand all that Elvis was saying, but I pieced his story together. The anthropologist stayed with Elvis while conducting his research. They hiked, ate, and drank beer together. "We were friends," he insisted. "He wanted to stay here, even after he finished asking his questions. These things," he gestured around the room, "belong to him."

"Where is he now?" I asked.

Elvis looked at me. "Dead," he said in a dull voice.

Frank Magna had died of cerebral malaria about a year before. Elvis had taken his body to Goroka, but no one came to claim him, so he arranged for transportation all the way to Moresby, where the French embassy finally assisted in transporting his remains.

I looked again at the dead man's possessions and felt a chill run through me. His things bore a lonely, detached air, the books warped; clothes molded and timeworn. I glanced at the violin case and remembered taking lessons myself ten years before, dwarfed by the awkward instrument, battling to keep it tucked beneath my chin. I remembered my fingers, stiff from a cold Wisconsin winter, wandering across the instrument's delicate neck, unable to find the notes as the bow faltered across the strings in an unending series of stutters.

Frank Magna's violin sat in despondent silence, warped by heat and rain, the black skin of its case peeling away into infinity.

"*Em nau*" Elvis' words cut into my thoughts, his voice triumphant. "There it is." He withdrew a book and crouched beside me. He opened a photo album and placed it on the split bamboo floor. Its images were faded, and a green and chemical tint seeped around the edges. The first pictures were of an excited-looking man in an airport.

"*Em ya,*" said Elvis, pointing at the man. "That's him." He looked thin and pale in the photographs, as if he were already sick. But despite his wasted appearance, I saw an exhilaration in him, unmarred by hesitation or uncertainty. Elvis stood to retrieve the whistling teapot, and I continued to look through the album.

In the photos that followed, I recognized Jackson's Airport in Moresby; Frank Magna stepping onto the tarmac, waiting in line at customs. He looked sweaty and tired, and I remembered how those hours on the airplane had sapped my energy until I staggered from the cabin's stale atmosphere into the bleached sunlight of the open sky, walking across roasting pavement in the thick swelter of a South Pacific afternoon.

Next came photos from the Highlands: Frank Magna riding in a crowded PMV, then crouching at the market before a display of *bilums*, then standing near a fire with Elvis, each of them gripping a bottle of SP beer. Knowing what became of him, I was struck by the intimacy of his photos. It felt like I was spying on him, watching him die.

I looked again at his possessions, discarded on a dirty floor on the far side of the world; undeniable testimony to his presence here, more distinct now that he was gone. The footprint of a man; all that remained of his best intentions.

Elvis handed me a tin mug of tea and shook his head. "These things are mine now, but I don't want them." He gestured as if they could disappear for all he cared. "He lived here with me. I took care of him. I was his friend. When he died, I got nothing."

I sipped the tea as Elvis told me how Frank Magna's mother had written letters to a nearby Christian mission, asking them to retrieve her son's things. "I tell them I want compensation, but they say no." He was almost pleading now. "Who can help me?"

I shook my head. "I don't know," I finally said. "Maybe one of the churches? Or the Red Cross? But it would be good for his family to have his things." I stood and handed him the remnants of my tea, eager to leave. "I need to go. My family is waiting for me."

Outside, the air had cooled and sweetened. The sun had begun to set, and its light poured like liquid gold across the gracefully reclining ranges, streaking the undersides of low clouds in furrows of pink and orange. I imagined the man's final hours in the dim interior of Elvis' hut, enfolded in the cold embrace of these same mountains, teetering on the precipice, here at the edge of the earth.

I arrived at Mari-eka a few minutes later and found Papa waiting for me.

"Aha-no will be here soon," he said, reminding me that we had planned to eat with the old man tonight. "Your Mama will go to her cousin's with Gilbert."

She called from within one of the nearby huts, "Nipi'e?" and I found immediate comfort in the sound of her voice.

"Mama," I answered.

"I'm happy you are home," she said.

Papa walked to the *singsing* ground, cupped his hands around his mouth and called a loud "whoo-ah" that echoed across the valley. "He will come soon," Papa said.

Back inside the hut, Papa asked about the day's training sessions and mentioned I had arrived late, a look of concern creeping across his face. "It's no good if you're late," he said. "Tomorrow you will wake up in time." He turned his head toward the back of the hut and called again at the top of his lungs. "Hoo-oh!"

A voice answered from behind our hut, "Whoa?"

Papa shouted rapidly in *tok ples*, and the voice responded. A minute later, Papa's brother Francis stuck his head into the hut. He entered and sat beside me. "Your Papa says you were late to your classes today," he said. "It's no good if you're late. Tomorrow, my children will sing in the morning, and you will know it is time to wake up. Yes?"

"*Em nau, kandre,*" I said. "Okay, Uncle."

"I have a truck," he announced as he stood, "if it starts, I will drive you." Then he added, with a hint of mischief, "It has no registration, so if we see the police, we'll have to run."

Thinking he was kidding, I played along. "*Em nau, kandre, bai mi halpim,*" I said cheerfully. "Okay, Uncle, I'll help."

For whatever reason, Francis thought this was very funny. His beard trembled as he laughed. "*Bai mi halpim,*" he repeated, and continued laughing as he left the hut. I could still hear his chuckle as he disappeared into the twilight.

Aha-no arrived later, wearing his yellow sweatshirt and grass skirt. Papa helped him to sit at the fire, and I stuttered answers to the usual questions about my health and comfort in the village. I told them about meeting Elvis that afternoon.

At hearing the name, the old man made a sour face. "Elvis is no good," he said in measured Pidgin. I asked if he had known Frank Magna, and he nodded. I told him what Elvis had told me and that he had asked for my help.

Aha-no gestured dismissively with his hand. "It's Elvis' worry. Forget it."

"He is a *bikhet*," Papa added. "No good. Stay away from him."

I asked Papa if Elvis was his brother, and he nodded and told me their fathers had been cousins. I thought about telling him that didn't make them brothers, but the specific terminology of blood relations was used interchangeably among Highlanders. If people were related, precisely how didn't matter. If you were from the same *lain*, you were siblings.

Aha-no rested his hand on my shoulder. "*Stori*," he said.

I asked what they wanted to know about, and they told me to talk about my family in the States. I went to the back of the hut and retrieved a small photo album from my duffel and brought to the fire. I placed it in Aha-no's thin hands, and he turned it over and around, examining the leather covering, the brass edgings around the corners, the stitching along the sides, approving of its quality. He opened it reverently and angled the photo toward the fire to catch its light.

He liked the picture of my father, and he and Papa leaned in for a closer view. Papa nodded approvingly. "He must have many wives," he said, his tone heavy with respect. I laughed, and so did they.

"Well, no," I said. "Just one."

"Only your Mama in America?" he asked, surprised.

"No, not my mother," I said. "My mother and father aren't together anymore."

Papa looked confused, but Aha-no understood, and his eyes turned sad again. He started to speak but changed his mind. He shook his head slowly and clucked his tongue a few times.

I turned to the next page, a picture of my mother rowing a canoe. "This is my mother."

"*Fit meri*," Papa pronounced.

They liked the photos of my brothers and me wearing tuxedos at my brother's wedding. They laughed when they noticed that all my brothers were taller than me. Papa shouted, "My boy is a runt!" and mussed my hair with his hand. I stood so that he had to stand on the tips of his toes to keep his hands on the top of my head.

"Yeah," I said, "a runt." And they laughed harder.

Next were photos of a couple of former girlfriends. "Amy," I said, pointing to one. She and I had dated in high school, and the picture in the album was her senior photo, a typical glamor shot, soft-lit, hazy around the edges. She was extremely pretty, with smooth, almost porcelain features. I'd never noticed before how alabaster the tone of her skin was. Papa clucked his tongue. "Nice," he said. "You will marry this one."

"Well, Papa, we aren't…" I began, intending to explain it didn't work that way in my culture. We had just learned the Pidgin word for cultural beliefs, *pasin*. I remembered it because it seemed to derive from the English word "passion," and with each day it was becoming increasingly evident just how great a passion the Papua New Guineans had for their cultural beliefs. "That's not the *pasin* of my people," I explained.

But Papa insisted. "You will pay bride price to her family. Not too much. I will talk to them," he said, pounding his fist to his chest.

I turned to the next page, to a picture of a girl I dated in college. "What about her?" I asked. In the photo, we had been camping, and she was wearing an old flannel shirt and a pair of dark sunglasses that hid her eyes. She held a long stick, which she had been using to stoke the fire.

"What is this one called?" asked Papa.

"Amy," I said. "Another Amy. A different girl."

Papa looked at me as if I had performed a miracle. Having dated two girls with the same name seemed to dramatically elevate his esteem for me. "Yes!" he exclaimed with glee. "And you will marry her, too!"

"Now, Papa," I began.

"Yes!" he said with delight. "The other one first, then this one. This is good!"

Aha-no didn't share Papa's awe, however, and remarked, "She looks like a *raskol*."

Papa and I turned back to the photo, and I saw what he meant. The dark glasses, the old shirt and the stick gave her a vaguely threatening look. Aha-no said, "She'll fight with your other wives. Marry this one last."

61

I laughed, Aha-no turned to the next photo, and Papa went back to preparing our dinner, still chuckling.

The next picture was of a place on Lake Michigan, not far from where I grew up, where some high school friends and I used to drive. Weather and waves over the course of millennia had carved dramatic cliffs along the shoreline. I had taken the picture during winter, when sheets of ice draped along the cliffs in much the same way the rainforest enveloped the mountains here, accommodating every contour. Aha-no squinted in the firelight, then looked at me, his eyebrows upturned, awaiting an explanation.

"Ice," I said, and he looked incredulous. It fascinated me to find that, while Aha-no could almost instantly digest the emotional complexity of something like my parents' divorce, an arrangement practically unheard of in the villages, he was nearly speechless with wonder at seeing something so simple as a wall of cliffs draped in ice. People, it seemed, lacked the capacity to surprise him. But this man, who had spent his entire life amid the magnificence of these mountain rainforests, could still find awe in the splendor of nature.

I began telling them about Wisconsin, how cold it was there. As we settled into our food and a chorus of crickets chirped just beyond the walls of the hut, I told them in simple, halting Pidgin, about a football game I had attended at Lambeau Field a few years earlier, on the day after Christmas. The temperature had dropped well below freezing before the game even started, and as it went on, it got a lot colder.

I savored telling the story, and I lingered as much as I could on each detail. Often, I couldn't come up with the right word in Pidgin for what I wanted to say, but Aha-no and Papa sat transfixed. I told them about the layers of clothes we wore, and I described the stadium, how many people were there. I talked about the rows of cars parked on the frigid lawns of houses near the stadium, and how the arctic wind carried the thundering sound of the crowd. Highlighting and embellishing details, I made grand, sweeping gestures when the words failed to come to me.

When I had finished, both Aha-no and Papa looked as if they harbored serious doubts about the truthfulness of the story but had enjoyed it, nevertheless. Both patted my shoulder and shook their heads in appreciation.

Then, Papa persisted in returning the topic to my future wife and/or wives, and I tried to turn the tables. "What about you, Papa?" I countered. "Why only one wife?"

He immediately responded, "That one is too much for me!"

We laughed again, but I persisted, "Why only one?"

Papa squatted beside me, and he and Aha-no shared a smile. "Once," Papa began, "after I was with your Mama, I brought back another. She was young and strong, and I would marry her, too, and have both wives to take care of me."

Aha-no grinned his gap-toothed grin at me and Papa continued. "I brought her to show her my village, to meet your Mama." He shook his head. "But your Mama was not happy to see her." His smile broadened. "They started to fight, those two," he gestured at the *singsing* ground.

"Your Mama was stronger," Papa said, and Aha-no nodded. "She beat the lady and chased her away." Then he shrugged. "She never came back. And I never brought home another one," Papa finished, a look of satisfaction on his broad face.

The evening went on, and the stories wandered with the smoke of the waning cooking fire. Aha-no told stories of his childhood, about the coming of the white man, automobiles, and roads. He shared his impressions, as a child, of the war. He remembered airplanes flying overhead as if by magic, and he heard fantastical tales of the white man's endless supplies of cargo, delivered by their flying machines. There remained something ethereal about it all, and even now he couldn't seem to separate the fable from the facts.

Aha-no was a gentle old man, and despite his frailty, or maybe in part because of it, he held a tremendous sense of dignity. He rarely raised his voice above a whisper; he didn't need to. He was delicate and unassuming, but behind the softness of his speech was an undeniable and immense authority.

As far as I knew, he held no official position. He would address the village often, holding aloft a crooked forefinger, but he was the antithesis of a politician. His ever-present gap-toothed smile bespoke the enigma of a greatly powerful yet implicitly fragile man, whose soft, trembling voice commanded the attention of assembled generations. When he spoke, a hush fell over his listeners, a silence borne of an earnest desire to partake of whatever bit of his wisdom and experience he chose to offer.

Our stories mingled with the smoke from the fire and drifted into the night, until I again dozed off. I was awakened by Aha-no shaking my knee, waving toward my sleeping bag. I rubbed my eyes and shook the hand he offered me. He clasped mine in both of his, smiling and looking me in the eye, wanting me to understand.

"*Nipi'e*," he said, "*gutpela stori.*" "Good stories."

I apologized again for my inabilities with his language, and he took one of his hands away from mine to wave it dismissively. "There is plenty of time," he assured me once again, maintaining a surprisingly firm grasp with his other hand. "Plenty of time."

I climbed beneath my mosquito net and into my sleeping bag. A light rain pattered on the roof of the hut, and as I drifted to sleep, I heard distant peals of thunder roaming through the dark and winding valleys.

In my sleepy contentment, I wondered if a storm was coming.

December 1, 1994 –Youth

Francis kept his promise, and the next morning I found myself coaxed awake by the distant sounds of his children singing from their own hut. By my count, Francis had five fidgety kids, from a toddler to a ten-year-old. No doubt one or two of them were among the group of gawkers who watched me at the stream the morning before. Now, I pictured them in the dim interior of their hut, performing a song handed down to them through generations of their forebears.

Their chorus was unrestrained by timidity, free of the awkward self-consciousness that would soon come with adolescence. Each voice was untrained, lyrical, and graceful, like the birdsongs that would soon resound from the surrounding trees. Together, they created a slow, sweet harmony that crept across the village grounds, filtered through our bamboo walls, and seeped into the confines of my mosquito net. They sang in the tribal language, and the sound held me spellbound. The village sat silent, as if entranced by the mysticism of that moment, except the occasional crow of a wandering rooster and the drone of the cicadas, a pulsing rhythm that complemented the performance.

Mama was already awake, stoking the fire while silently mouthing the lyrics of the song. "Hurry," she said when she saw me move. "It's no good if you're late. Francis will drive you."

Papa yawned, scratching the ridges of his bare belly. "Aha-no was happy to *stori* with you last night," he told me. "People will ask about you, and he will tell them you are doing well." I smiled and waved as I ducked out the door.

Beyond the gate, Francis stood beside an old and dented pale-yellow Daihatsu. It too had a wire grate bolted over its cracked windshield, coated with dry, opaque mud.

He gestured to the front seat. "*Calapim,*" he said. "Climb in."

He turned the key, and nothing happened. He sucked his teeth and smacked the steering column, and the truck shuddered with the impact. He tried the key again and the engine groaned to life. Grinning, he slapped his chest and boasted, "I'm a mechanic!" Then he threw the car into gear and we ground our way to the bridge, where the pig, Wilbur, scampered out of our way.

The trail had been uncomfortable enough in the Peace Corps' Land Cruiser, but it was much worse in Francis' truck. His suspension was shot, and the uneven road surface vibrated along the chassis through the seats, worn nearly to their metal frames. My spine compressed with every bump, and the springs under what remained of the cushions jabbed at my legs.

As we negotiated a hairpin turn at an overlook, I watched a cloud-bank snaking its way along the basin a few miles to the west. The mantle of precipitation nestled between the steep ridges, obscuring everything below it. It was at a lesser elevation than us, and I watched from above as the heavy gray mist withdrew along the darkly wooded riverbed, skulking off toward Daulo Pass. Soon, the morning sun would spill across the valley and wash away the remnants of cloud, bathing the woods in fluid sunlight.

It rained almost every night, and each morning, as daylight worked its way through the leaves and branches to heat the forest floor, the precipitation lifted in translucent curtains of ghostly vapor, filtering through the canopy to drift skyward like an apparition ascending from the primal morass.

As we bounced along, Francis pointed out sights of local interest. He showed me where the hut in which he was born once stood, though it had been put to the torch in a tribal war years ago. He gossiped about the man whose wife had run away with a PMV driver from the *nambis*, or coast, and the woman who had lost four children to illnesses and accidents and now worked her garden alone, refusing to speak to anyone.

Particularly notable was an elaborate hut, complete with electric lights strung from a diesel generator. The hut belonged to a man who collected and sold manure and called himself "Mr. Shit." He drove a weather-beaten red truck with the words, "Chickenshit, Horseshit, Cowshit– but no Bullshit" on the side, and he was one of the most respected businessmen in the area. Francis said he was considering a run for parliament.

Bouncing along the trail with my elbow propped on the open window, I allowed the incense of the Highland morning to fill my lungs. I felt cleansed by the increasingly familiar aromas of wet grass and mud, sweet, ripe bananas, wood smoke, and the spiced scent of betel nut, called *buai* in Pidgin.

Buai comes from the tall, slender *areca* palm tree found in abundance throughout the tropical Pacific. The nuts are harvested in clusters and sold to be chewed with mustard and lime. The nut itself is about the size of a walnut, but with a fibrous green husk. The chewer tears away the skin and bites into the nut, then adds a stalk of *daka*, or mustard, and a pinch of *kambang*, a powdered lime mixture made from incinerated coral. The *daka* and *kambang* extract an alkaloid in the *buai* that creates a mild narcotic effect on the chewer.

Papua New Guineans chew *buai* everywhere they go; in their gardens, on PMVs, at village meetings and ceremonies. Many believe it cures illnesses, freshens breath, and straightens teeth, none of which is true. In fact, the chewers' teeth become stained with red mucus, then blackened by decay before falling out, and even then, many continue to "chew" *buai* by grinding the mixture in a mortar before putting it in their mouths.

The mixture turns the saliva bright red, and chewers spit indiscriminately. Throughout the country, red stains dot the streets and footpaths like insidious pools of blood. Everywhere I went, the air held a trace of the citric aroma of *kambang*, as it did that morning, in the back of Francis' truck.

At Kefamo, Barry sat in a small office, which was sparsely decorated with a metal desk and a wall map of the area around surrounding Goroka. The map was dotted with flagged pins to represent the villages where volunteers were placed. Barry was leaning back in a chair, his sandaled feet on the desk, reading a U.S. newspaper with a dateline from a month ago. He pored over it as if the news had occurred just the night before.

I knocked, and he looked over the top of the paper. "What's up, my man?"

"I wanted to ask you about something," I said. "Did you know a guy named Frank Magna?"

There was recognition in Barry's face, but little emotion, which was uncommon for him. He seemed to have strong feelings about everything, positive or negative. He didn't strike me as one to anything by small measures. But in this case, he registered only mild surprise. His eyebrows arched, he pushed up his glasses and he shook his head.

"I wouldn't say I *knew* him," he said. "I knew *of* him, heard stories about him."

I asked if he knew about his death, and he said he did. Then he leaned back in his chair, studying the ceiling. "He was a strange bird," he said, exhaling at length. "He really wanted to be a part of it all. Did all the things the villagers do: worked the gardens, chewed *buai*, partied," he said, significantly. "At some of the trade stores along the Highway, they throw these wild soirées they call 'six to sixes', meaning they start at six in the evening and go 'til six in the morning. It gets crazy: booze, girls, fights. He liked to go to those."

Now Barry dropped his sandaled feet to the floor and the soles of his sandals slapped against the linoleum as he leaned on the desk. "He missed something though, ah?" he said. "As much as the people in his village cared about him, he was still an outsider. He wasn't one of them. I don't think he realized that."

"But he didn't expect to die up here," I said, and paused. "It sounds. .. lonely."

He shrugged. "Death's a lonely prospect. But he felt like he was where he belonged."

I scratched my chin and looked at the newspaper. At the bottom, I saw scores from football games I remembered being shown on the TV above the bar where I worked before leaving the States. It already seemed impossible that was just a few weeks ago.

"Does it bother you, to be where he was?" Barry asked.

"No," I responded. "But yesterday I met the guy he lived with. He's a brother or cousin or something of my host father."

I told Barry about Elvis hoarding Frank Magna's possessions. When I finished, Barry nodded. "I hadn't heard about that," he said, though he didn't seem surprised.

"Well, I feel like I should do something," I said. "He has this guy's journals, his pictures, stuff his family would want. And he asked me what he should do with it."

"Sure," he nodded. "You're a white man, he's been told white men know more than him, so he thinks you know how to get him what he wants."

"Maybe I could get him to give the stuff back," I said.

"Maybe," he conceded "But if you convince him to do that, and he doesn't get what he wants out of it, now you're involved. What do you do then?"

I sat back to pick at the clumps of mud that had wedged into the soles of my hiking boots. "I don't like not doing anything," I said.

"It's up to you. But you can't take on something like this part way. If you get involved, you get involved entirely." He paused. "You gotta remember why you're here."

I flashed through the ambiguities of what brought me to this place. "What if I don't know why I'm here?" I asked, which brought the Cheshire-cat grin back to Barry's face.

After he chuckled, I asked, "What about you? Why are you here?"

Barry laced his fingers atop his head, his eyes drifting along the edges of the newspaper. He seemed unprepared to answer, as if it never even occurred to him to wonder. "Baseball," he finally stated, and he seemed content to leave it at that.

"Baseball," I repeated. Then he nodded, so I nodded, and then I said, "I don't get it."

Barry was born in 1950 in Phillipsburg, New Jersey. His hometown was less than a hundred miles from Tunkhannock, where I was born twenty years later.

"I played baseball," he said, "and it was my life, ah? Only thing that mattered to me. I started Little League a year early, played for my high school team, captain of the team, matter of fact. I was good," he said. "I had designs on going pro."

Coming from someone else, that would have sounded like a boast, but

69

there was something disarming in the way Barry said it. He had no expectation of what it might mean to me. It was a simple statement, and he gave it no more weight than he would if he were telling me where he went to grade school or the name of his best friend when he was seven. They were nothing more than pieces of the puzzle.

Baseball introduced Barry to the world outside his hometown. The U.S. in those days was still segregated, even in the north. The only people Barry knew who weren't white were the kids he met playing baseball. But he got along better with the black kids than he did with the white ones. He related to them better. They made more sense to him. He wasn't the type to give it much thought– that's just the way it was.

He barely finished high school. "Graduated two hundred and ninety second out of a class of 293," and now he did appear to be bragging, seeming almost to envy the one person who finished behind him.

He couldn't have made it to college on his grades, but he found himself fielding scholarship offers because of his skill as a baseball player. "Any jock could go to college," he said. "So here I was, barely a high school graduate, but I'm shopping colleges, while most of the guys I played ball with were going to war."

This was 1968; the year my own father was finishing a twelve-month tour as a combat engineer in Vietnam. Dad came home to a country that was losing its patience and losing its way. Barry knew what was happening; he watched Walter Cronkite every night. College would have kept him out, but others, guys he had grown up with and played baseball with, didn't have that option. If they had to go, why shouldn't he?

"Besides," he admitted, "I was curious." He wanted to see a war.

So he turned down the scholarship offers, went to the draft board, and requested his name be moved to the top of the list. "Didn't enlist, mind you," he pushed up his glasses. "That would've meant a three-year commitment. I didn't want that."

So, he arranged to be drafted. But the army, with the timeless and byzantine wisdom of an established bureaucracy, sent him to Europe and trained him as a radio operator, monitoring Eastern Bloc communications. The boredom drove him half-insane, and he constantly lobbied for a transfer to Southeast Asia. That fit, too. Barry was just about the only person trying to get into a war so many others were trying to get out of.

But good things, as they say, come to those who wait, and eventually he got his wish. In 1970, at the age of twenty, he went to Vietnam. He was stationed in Chu Lai, a Marine and Army infantry base a hundred kilometers southeast of Da Nang, on the coast of the South China Sea.

"What do you say about it?" he continued. "Sex, drugs, the Beatles and Vietnam taught me how the world worked."

Strange as it seemed, he enjoyed his war. He liked the intensity, and he loved the Vietnamese people. He had made sergeant in Europe, so he now commanded a squad of fifteen men. They thought he was fearless, and maybe he was, he conceded. "When we weren't working, we were chasing prostitutes or smoking grass." He shook his head. "It wasn't a bad life."

After his tour, he went home and enrolled in junior college, then college at Florida State. "I bounced between jobs for a few years, but I could never quite get comfortable back in the States. All the bullshit," he said. "War teaches you everything you ever want to know about power – who's got it and who doesn't. Now I couldn't get past it. When Reagan got elected, I said 'enough, I'm out.'" He joined the Peace Corps.

He spent two years in the Solomon Islands and stayed after he finished, working with aid and development organizations. A few years later, he drifted west to Papua New Guinea, and he'd been here ever since.

"I love this place," he said, and his eyebrows arched over his glasses. "It's magic."

That afternoon, over a card game, Brent said, "You guys wouldn't believe the rodent in my hut last night," holding his hands a foot apart. Holding a cigarette clutched between two fingers, his gestures left trails of smoke that circled him like a specter. "It woke me up, but I was afraid to do anything, 'cause if it came down to me against him, I'm pretty sure he could've taken me."

"Please," Dieter said dismissively, "a little mouse?" And he placed the palms of his hands a few inches apart. "That's nothing. I woke up a few nights ago at about three in the morning because I could hear a rat in *my*

71

hut." And how he spread his hands apart, suggesting the rat in question was about the size of a housecat, and glanced sideways at Brent. "But that's no big deal, right? They're in there all the time, huge ones, size of a PMV. Except it turned out this one was inside my mosquito net, going after my foot!" Dieter's tone replayed his panic, and we started to laugh.

"I shit you not. So, I go *nuts*, right? Yelling and screaming," he shouted. "I can feel it squirming at my feet and I keep kicking it up in the air, and it's squealing and it keeps flipping into my mosquito net and then rolling back down, and I kick it back up again like a pinball or some goddamn thing, and so then my host family wakes up, and they freak out, because they don't know what the hell's going on, and they all gather around, and I can hear them yelling, and I just keep shouting 'Rat! Rat! Rat!' over and over again, and I don't know if they can hear it squeaking over my yelling, but it's this crazy trap I can't get out of, and it seems to go on for so long, until my whole mosquito net comes down from the ceiling, and me and the rat are tangled up in the net and my sleeping bag, rolling around on the floor, and I still don't know where the goddamn thing is, so I just keep kicking and swinging."

I stopped laughing long enough to say, "Man, I would have paid top dollar to see that."

"When I got untangled, the rat was gone," he finished, his intensity fading. "My family never even saw it." Calm now, he began dealing the cards.

"Wuss." This came from another volunteer, Mike.

Mike was an enigma. A great tall, hulking kid with an imposing physical presence, he rarely spoke. During training sessions, he would rest one elbow on his knee, chin between thumb and forefinger, listening intently but saying little. He admitted the world had become a more confusing place over the past few weeks, but he was okay with it – it made him laugh. Everything made him laugh. The whole experience just seemed funny to him. It would have been infuriating if he didn't include himself among the things he found ridiculous and hilarious. But he was self-effacing and always had a new story about his own missteps.

He came from a suburb of Chicago, where his parents still lived in the oak-paneled home they bought before he was born. A product of Catholic schools, he had attended the same Catholic university from which both of his parents and his sister graduated. Mike, like me, had since lapsed in his Catholicism; he never quite felt like he fit in at church, or anywhere else. He joined the Peace Corps to define himself in contrast to his culture, and to set himself apart from it in some way. He didn't expect to make the world a better place. It would be nice, he admitted, but he wasn't counting on it.

Now, he pointed to Dieter. "That's why our families think we're high maintenance. They already think we can't so much as take leak without getting lost, falling, or catching dengue fever," he flipped a card on the table, and then gestured to me. "Speaking of which, my family told me about your little wipe-out going down the hill to wash the other day."

"It wasn't a hill," I clarified. "It was a cliff. I had to rappel down to take a bath."

Brent laughed, and I turned on him. "Okay, well, at least *I* slipped in the mud," I told him. "I heard from my family that *you* tripped over a tree root that has undoubtedly been there longer than you've been alive. You had to grow to a twenty-two-year-old man-child and travel halfway around the world just to find this thing and fall over it."

"The worst part is," he agreed, "now every time I go on a hike with my family, they point out every little bump and tree root they see, so I won't trip over that, too."

We had all heard stories about each other from our host families. Another volunteer from our group, named Jerry, had achieved mythical status in his village and throughout the affiliated tribes, due to the volume of his snoring, which could only be described as astonishing. Mike had shared a room with Jerry at the teachers college in Moresby, so he was already well accustomed, but Jerry's host family in the Highlands had not been adequately prepared. They, of course, said nothing about it, but they ended up building him a separate hut, because of the noise. And every morning in his new, private residence, Jerry awoke to the sound of dogs, growling and digging at the base of the hut, trying to get in to tear apart whatever monster was making that awful noise.

My host family found the situation very funny, and Papa took delight in describing the sleep-deprived exhaustion of Jerry's family.

We exchanged stories and abuse, scrutinizing our anxieties and failures. It provided a kind of affirmation, a relief found only in *schadenfreude*. Ostensibly we were just telling stories, but we had also found an avenue to channel what we were experiencing. Things that seemed so intense in our villages somehow became indescribably funny here. We made light of each other's misfortunes, celebrated the absurd, because we found familiarity there. And we hurried to get it off our chests before going back to acquire more.

Our conversation grew louder and faster as the words and insults flowed, and the speed of our card game increased to keep pace. The rounds flew, and we slapped the cards onto the table with greater flourish, building to a crescendo of shouting and card throwing.

When I looked at my watch, it read 5:00. "That's it for me, girls," I said. "Time for me to go."

We exchanged threats of a rematch and denigrated one another's card-playing prowess and general masculinity, and we stepped outside to find a thick layer of dark cloud creeping across the valley to settle among the forested mountains. A breeze blew with an almost imperceptible chill, the air ominous, electric. It would take an hour to get to Mari-eka, but the rain would be here before that.

"Great," I lamented. "I don't have my raincoat, and I'm gonna get soaked."

"I have one you can borrow," Mike said, pulling a green military-type poncho from his *bilum*. "Here."

I gaped and asked, "You keep your raincoat wrapped in a tent?"

"This *is* my raincoat."

"Are you serious?" I asked, regarding at it again. "I could fit that over my car."

"Take it or leave it," he said, as the first thunderclap roiled down the valley.

The PMV came just in time. A few minutes into the ride, the skies opened, and the rain came in a deafening rattle, like marbles poured onto the roof. The enormity of the sound overwhelmed the others passengers' curiosity about a white man in a PMV, so I sat nearly unnoticed on an unevenly hinged bench seat, my view obscured by cascading water.

Shapes and colors lost their distinctness in the downpour. The extremities of the trees and hills faded, as each seemed to blur into the next, deconstructing the landscape to an unfocused, amorphous mass. Thick clouds blotted out the sun, and the leaves became such a deep shade of emerald they looked almost black. The mud of the footpaths shone as a blaze-orange hue against the surrounding gray-blue-greens.

The windows were cinched shut, but water flitted through gaps in the door frames and floorboards. The smell of exhaust fumes, smoke and sweat became more pronounced in the sultry air, and moisture clung in a film to the windows.

I felt just as drawn to the world outside those windows as the condensation was, pulled toward the panes and what lay beyond. I wanted to be engulfed, subsumed, purified, baptized by the rain. It seemed like nothing could be more natural than to let the rain rinse away the noxious fumes and body odors of the PMV.

As we approached the trade store at the trail-head, I pulled out Mike's poncho and called for the driver to stop. He eased to the side of the road, and I struggled over the other passengers. I dropped a few coins into his hand, climbed out and began trudging up the muddy path.

Runoff tumbled from the hills in rivulets that dug channels into the surface of the trail, eroding the clay that covered the stones along its length.

I passed an old woman standing in a garden, her back stooped, wiry arms and legs working the thick mud. She had on a long, dirty skirt, its hem rustling with the flow of water. Instead of a *meri* blouse, she wore a faded Bob Marley t-shirt, and he too stared at me from her sunken chest, a huge spliff jutting from the corner of his mouth. She and Bob watched me pass, both unperturbed by the rain. I waved, but she didn't respond.

I must have I looked strange to her, as I leaned into the incline and stumbled up the path, lost in Mike's oversized poncho, and the rain sputtered against me. Neither of us spoke, but I couldn't disengage her stare or penetrate the intensity of her focus to find its motivation. Her look wasn't one of surprise or curiosity or bemusement, like the stares of the others I'd grown accustomed to receiving here. She couldn't be bothered with trivialities and surface appearances. She seemed to want to cut straight to the heart of the matter, to find its essence.

I wondered what she hoped to discover in me, but I suppose she may have pondered the same about me. I was "the other" to her, as much as she was to me. So, what did we seek in each other? Was it the same thing? Some way of better defining and understanding ourselves, reflected in the incongruity of the other? Did each of us wonder if the other knew something, or had something, that we ourselves didn't?

The trail became a river of mud, and I braced against the embedded stones to jump from one to the next, causing the water to leap and scatter. As the slope steepened, the runoff and mud flowed faster, carrying with it more of the trail's surface. My boots became covered and heavy with sodden clay.

Through the rainfall, I heard a child's voice, then another, and I heard the word '*masta*' followed by laughter. The voices came from behind me, and I turned to see two kids scurry into the bush. I heard giggles as I hovered, balanced on the rocks. On impulse, I picked up a handful of mud and tossed it into the bushes, causing hysterical laughter. Then a clump of mud flew toward me. I charged the bushes and the kids stood, shirtless, shoeless, the water streaming down their bare bellies, each with a handfull of mud. I pivoted to run in the other direction, and they gave chase, hooting and laughing. I scooped another handful of mud and threw it at them, and they returned fire.

We carried on a running battle, as I chased the kids, sending them leaping into the undergrowth that fringed the path. We moved along the trail, the rain showing no signs of easing, and more kids joined. Soon, there were fifteen or twenty of them chasing me and each other along the slick path, all of us slinging mud as quickly as we could. Sometimes, they gathered to conspire in a collective attack, and I rushed from the bushes through the middle of the group, watching them scatter before me, hurling gobs of mud.

The finale came when my foot got tangled in Mike's poncho and I stumbled headfirst into a deep puddle of water and mud, causing a tidal wave to sweep across the trail. The kids laughed with renewed enthusiasm and gathered to watch me pull myself up to my hands and knees, dazed. I splashed water at them, and they splashed back.

This was how Papa and Francis found me, after setting out in Francis' truck, afraid I was lost in the rain. They had just rounded a bend and come upon the puddle, with me in the middle, surrounded by shrieking children. Papa leapt from the car and shouted at the kids, who again scattered into the bushes, now filled with genuine fear.

Papa helped me up, apologizing, but I shook my head and wiped the mud from my hands. "It's okay, Papa. We were just playing." I pulled down the hood of the poncho and leaned my head back to let the rain rinse my face. Papa stared at me, confused.

"The rain has washed you too much," Francis said, shaking his head. "Your papa and I will take you home," and Papa turned again to scowl at the kids.

Francis' truck failed to restart, so he popped the hood and fidgeted with the battery as the downpour continued around us. As I peered over his shoulder into the engine block, a clump of mud smacked me in the back, and I turned in amazement to find that Papa had already reloaded and was about to throw another. I dodged just in time, and the mud hit Francis, causing him to jerk his head suddenly and smack it on the raised hood.

The game was back on.

That night, as I lay in my sleeping bag, my knee throbbed where I had hit it when I fell. It was a dull, oddly pleasant ache– the kind that causes just enough discomfort to remind you that you're alive, and to rejoice in the simple coincidence of your existence. I felt heavy and relaxed as I listened to the muffled sounds of the falling rain slapping against the roof, causing the stalks of thatched grass to flinch with each impact. Inside, we were warm and dry, and the sputtering flame from the kerosene lamp cast a gentle illumination through the soft darkness, just enough for me to read my book.

I lifted my head to look around the interior of the hut, our hut, and I realized I hadn't felt this good in a very long time.

December 8, 1994 – Faith

Papa's brother Francis lived behind us, at the foot of an embankment. His hut sat amid a cluster of narrow gum trees whose delicate branches housed an extended family of lorikeets. The screeching of the birds mingled with the songs, taunts, and laughter of Francis' children to create an unceasing din of commotion and activity that drifted up the hill and into our hut. This dissonant surge gave voice to the village itself, especially in the early mornings, with so few other sounds to compete with it.

Along with his kids, a few chickens and a skinny, flea-bitten mutt called Bobby, Francis also had a goat. I never knew why. I don't think he milked her, and he seemed too emotionally attached to consider making a meal of her. He treated her more like a pet than anything, though I never heard him call her by name. He just called her "stupid goat" in a soft voice as he nudged her with his toe. But any time I visited Francis' hut, I would find the goat there, perched on a hummock in unconcerned solitude, or tied with a length of twine to the doorframe to prevent her from foraging in the garden. She would chew on stray bamboo from the wall or doze peacefully in the doorway, ears flicking at the flies. There was hardly any reason to pay much attention to the goat– until one morning, when Francis awoke to find she'd been killed.

Each day had found me settling more deeply into the calm certainty of the routine of village life. It began in the pale light of daybreak, as villagers eased into their mornings, mulling over cooking fires, drinking cups of tea and rubbing backs and knees made sore by crouching over *kau kau* mounds or lifting restless children. Sitting before the hearth of their cooking fires, they allowed the cool morning air to seep from their joints as slowly as the dew evaporated from the roofs of their huts.

Something felt different on that morning. An unsettling fever filled the air, waking everyone and spurring them to motion. In our hut, embers smoldered in the fire pit, but no one was there. Outside, people chattered and hustled with nervous anxiety. I pulled on a shirt and ducked through the doorway to find a crowd gathered beside Francis' hut, and I walked down to join them.

When he saw me, Francis motioned me forward, and the crowd parted to reveal the goat lying on her side, tongue hanging from her open mouth, eyes glossy. Her chest had been cut open, and a cluster of insects swarmed around the innards, which gleamed in the first rays of the morning sun. Francis stood flanked by his children, who grasped his waist and stared at the dead animal. Shirtless and dusty, they looked bored, their faces empty of emotion, staring at the goat as they would any piece of raw meat.

The flies offended Francis, and he waved a palm frond over the carcass to shoo them away. But the agitation only temporarily diverted them. They would almost immediately return to the exposed viscera, until the frond whisked them away again.

"They killed my goat," he said to no one in particular.

He normally brought the goat inside for the night, but he told us that as he turned in the previous night, he sensed from the dry and still air that it wouldn't rain, so he left her outside. He had spent all day driving his truck to and from the markets around Goroka, delivering passengers and cargo, and he fell asleep in the early evening and slept through the night, which was unusual for him. Normally, at least one of the kids would wake him, crying for a drink of water or fighting with a sibling. But that night, he slept without interruption. When he awoke that morning, he stepped out to fetch a bucket for tea and found the dead goat.

I asked, "Why would somebody do that?" and he swung the palm frond vehemently.

"*No save*," he said. "I don't know."

Mama called to me from the crowd. "Nipi'e!" she said. "You have your school." She had taken to calling my training sessions at Kefamo "school." "This is not your worry," she told me. "It's time for you to go."

79

I noticed again that none of the villagers were paying any attention to me, and this suddenly seemed so unusual as to be unsettling. Tim gripped my arm and for once, there was no smile on his face as he looked through narrowed eyes.

"This is no good." He gestured at the goat. "Spirits are not quiet."

"What?" I asked.

"This is *sanguma*," he answered. Witchcraft.

I looked over his shoulder at the goat. "Magic?" I said, doubt in my voice.

"Why didn't our uncle, our *kandre*, wake up?" Tim asked. I began to answer, but he cut me off, his eyes wide. "They kept Francis asleep."

"Why?" I asked.

He shook his head. "A warning, maybe," he said. "Or some payback. But spirits were here, and they are unhappy."

At Kefamo a few hours later, I told Barry and the others about the goat and Tim's explanation. We sat in the remote tranquility of the conference room as a cool breeze worked through the window louvers. It felt a thousand miles from the village.

"There was nothing magic about it," I said. "But somebody killed that goat and left it there. What does that mean?"

Barry said it might have been retribution against Francis or someone else in the village. A redress for a slight or an offense, an attempt to find balance. He asked if I was worried.

I shrugged and asked, "Should I be?"

"Not about yourself," he answered. "If someone's got a beef against your uncle, or even against your village, they won't hold it against you. There are rules surrounding the pursuit of grievances. Bystanders are bystanders. It's got nothing to do with you, not your worry; you aren't involved in relationships between villages and tribes."

But as I had grown more comfortable in my place in the village, I had felt an increasing sense of kinship with the people there. I didn't want to be pushed aside. I was supposed to be learning from them, and about them. I couldn't do that from outside. I remembered again Mama's insistence that morning that I leave the village.

Now, Barry prepared to settle into one of his talks. We had spent enough time with him to recognize the way he pursued his role as our teacher. The constant activity that occupied his mind manifested itself physically, even when he wasn't speaking. He rarely sat still. Instead, he paced or fidgeted with his glasses, anything to cope with his surfeit of energy. When he spoke, his thoughts tumbled forth in a rush, each hard on the heels of the one before it. He never used notes, never seemed prepared. If he didn't have a topic in mind, he'd allow one to establish itself, and he would talk about it from the top of his head, allowing it to follow its own direction as it worked its way through his mind.

"Listen," he pointed at each of us. "I've said this before. *Sanguma* is real. It's not a question of whether you believe there are spirits out there committing acts of sorcery, or not. The people here believe in it so strongly the government has written legislation outlawing its practice. Sorcery is a prosecutable offense in this country."

A few chuckled, others just gaped. "That's insane," someone said.

"Not necessarily." Barry shrugged. "By offering a legal venue for the pursuit of complaints against black magic, it reduces the likelihood of villagers taking matters into their own hands." He looked around the room. "You've gotta take this seriously, 'cause you *will* come across it."

"How do we to take it seriously?" asked Dieter. His voice bore an edge of hesitation as it traveled through the thick afternoon air, heavy with impending rain. "I'm all for respecting traditional beliefs. But in a couple of months I'll be teaching high school science. How do I reconcile this with science? This is the way the villagers explain what they consider unexplainable: why is the sky blue, how does an airplane fly? They call it magic because they don't have a better answer, and I can understand that. But I do have a better answer. That's the whole reason I'm here."

"Just don't be surprised if they don't accept your answer," said Barry. "They can repeat it back to you – they're good at telling you what you want to hear – but that doesn't mean they believe it. This isn't about a preponderance of evidence. It's about faith and tradition. You can tell them whatever you want, but you can't assume they'll accept what you say. They pick and choose what they believe in, just like you do."

"Except I don't pick and choose what I believe," I said. "I believe something because it's been demonstrated to be true."

What frustrated me was that it seemed condescending to defer to the misconceptions of tradition if we knew otherwise, simply on the assumption that the villagers were incapable of accepting something that fell outside of their system of beliefs. There are absolutes in life. Truth isn't always clouded by degree and relativity.

"The people in your village don't want to debate this with you," Barry continued. "They know you don't believe what they believe, so they'll avoid discussing it with you. You will only be allowed so far into the depths of this society."

"But in that case," I said, "if we'll never be a part of the most intrinsic institutions here, what's the harm in taking a subjective view of them? It's acceptable for us as Westerners to detail the failings of our own way of doing things – in fact, it's a civic responsibility – so why is it not okay to point out the shortcomings of theirs? It seems patronizing, to shield the Highlanders from scrutiny because they are a poorer society."

Yet when I looked beyond the pitiful end of Francis' goat, I could also concede that how she died didn't matter. The villagers didn't have to know definitively how something happened; only that it happened. What made the crops grow didn't matter, as long as they grew. Why force people to reject one belief in favor of another, when neither would ultimately influence the way they live their lives? Maybe imposing quantifiable explanations on the Highlanders wouldn't benefit them. Maybe it would only serve to gratify those who had come to "develop" them.

I knew there was some of that in me too, that at least in part I was serving myself, rather than the people who lived here. But I wanted to fight that impulse. I wanted to serve a greater purpose. I wanted to find a way to be selfless.

Barry sensed our uncertainty. "Nobody expects you to give up your principles," he said. "If you want to inquire about their beliefs, even try to influence them, it's up to you, but it will complicate things more than you can imagine."

"But aren't the traditional beliefs sort of fading away, anyway?" Brent asked. "Most of the people in my village are Seventh Day Adventists. They go to church every day, and they never talk about magic."

"Not to you," Barry responded. "But if it came down to it, you might be surprised."

Outside, a band of clouds made their way across the sky, dragging long shadows across the ridges and treetops, through the window louvers, pools of darkness creeping across the faded wooden floors.

Christianity arrived in the Highlands right alongside the first Westerners. In the wake of the Leahy expedition came hordes of Evangelicals, Catholics, Baptists and Pentecostals. The missionaries saw a blank canvas; countless lost souls waiting to meet their god. They came in droves and made themselves as much a part of the landscape as the diesel trucks that slogged through the mud behind them, lugging machinery, Bibles, money and alcohol, the cargo that would transform this part of the world.

Western religion was at immediate odds with beliefs in *sanguma* and black magic. "In the days before the missionaries," Barry told us, "the indigenous societies had their own intricate framework of spiritual beliefs. But now," he shook his head, "they say more than ninety five percent of the population has converted to Christianity. Many of the old beliefs have gone by the wayside. At least, in essence," he clarified, removing his glasses to wipe them on his shirt, "but not in entirety."

It was not a simple transition, he assured us. "In the old days, the missionaries treated this place as a misguided backwater. They used to say the souls of the natives were black because they didn't know God. They told 'em that's why their skin was black." He raised his eyebrows and shook his head. "They intimidated and browbeat people into converting to the white man's religion."

I stared around the room at the others, slumped into folding chairs, cracked and dirty bare feet crossed over sunburned and scratched legs, stubbled chins perched on fists, eyelids sloped like the louvers on the windows. This was only half-real to us.

"And Highlanders are agreeable people," Barry continued. "It's not polite to disagree with a guest, even if he's full of shit. So, a missionary comes to you, you welcome him, carry his stuff, make him comfortable. He asks, 'Do you accept Jesus Christ as your savior', and you do the polite thing and say, 'Sure,' even if you don't know or care who Jesus Christ is. They bribed the villagers with food, clothing, medicine, tools, and trinkets just to lure them into church. Then they guilted them into staying and converting. And if this was the entirety of the missionaries' influence here, it would be easy to dismiss them. But it's not."

Now he leaned back, his voice serious. "Those same missionaries taught people to read and to write. They introduced lifesaving inoculations, taught the importance of hydration for babies with diarrhea, dramatically reducing infant mortality. They taught the prevention and treatment of malaria, the biggest killer in this part of the world. In many villages, if kids weren't educated by missionaries, they weren't educated at all – there was no one else to do it. The missionaries were, and still are, in the remotest places in the Highlands, teaching agricultural techniques and water sanitation, delivering and implementing programs that elevate the health and quality of life of the people there."

Still, I couldn't get over the incongruity of it. It seemed absurd to attach religion to the distribution of material goods, as a lure or as a threat. Food, medicine, schools, and houses; those things have nothing to do with spirituality or faith. If you combine the two to coerce converts, doesn't that cast into doubt the sincerity of the conversion? If someone offers a glass of water to a man dying of thirst, but only on the condition he accept Christ as his savior, then he'll accept Christ as his savior, but not because he sought that faith – when the water is gone, his faith is gone with it. By manipulating people with trinkets and guilt, the conversion becomes incidental.

As our conversation continued, I felt anew the sense of hypocrisy and cynicism I had come to associate with my Catholic upbringing. I thought about the hours I spent in the oppressive silence of our church in Green Bay, about the fear and guilt I found to be inherent in Christianity. I remembered the pale congregants of our little chapel on the Fox River, and I tried to envision them hacking through rainforests and bug-infested swamps with a machete in one hand and a Bible in the other.

My mother played piano for the church choir, and my father sat on the vestry, the council that administered the church's finances. We went to Mass every week, and while much of the congregation dispersed immediately after the service to watch the Packer game, my parents lingered over coffee and stale donuts, dissecting the homily with those few diehards for whom God still outranked football.

Our religion confused and depressed me, with its morbid images of a beaten and tortured martyr and the constant reminder that I was somehow responsible for his suffering. I never understood the shame and guilt that were imprinted on me in stilted, archaic language. I remember church as droning, echoing sermons, the heavy aromas of incense and candle wax, sickly sweet altar wine and stale communal bread. Itchy sweaters, chafing collars, the pervasive sense of mortality and doom, a bizarre, fetishistic obsession with sin, torment, blood, and death. I was a kid, daydreaming of girls and adventure, fantasizing about the world beyond the Midwest, and my religion seemed to insist I ignore my curiosity and suppress my instincts.

Yet as stifling as that repression was, I sensed at the same time a kinship I genuinely admired. In spite of itself, our church seemed a happy place, a bizarre combination of tyranny and joy.

But that was a mirage, a cloak, a veneer of contentment, and it dissolved when I was fourteen and my parents got divorced. Catholics stay married, even if they're miserable – especially if they're miserable. To my ongoing disbelief and profound shame, even after my parents split up, our family continued going to Mass every Sunday, Mom and Dad situating them-selves at opposite sides of the congregation, the kids switching back and forth, one week with Mom, one with Dad. Through whispers and furtive glances, the community made it clear they were discomforted by our pres-ence, while I agonized beneath the unwanted attention that I had spent my life trying to avoid.

Eventually, the church council removed Dad from the vestry and encour-aged Mom to leave the choir, to be replaced by a noticeably less talented, but safely married, musician.

This ridiculous place, with its boasts of community and support, of standing alongside its neighbors in their time of greatest need, wanted nothing to do with us in ours. As my family fell apart and five scared kids sought some comfort, some reassurance that things might turn out okay for us, we realized our church offered nothing of the kind. Catholicism became another piece of Green Bay I couldn't wait to leave behind.

Yet Barry, no less a skeptic than me, remained persistent in his praise. "The missionaries dedicate their lives to this country," he continued. "They care deeply about the people here. They spend their entire lives here, and they're buried out there in those jungles." He paused, then raised his eyebrows. "And you have more in common with them than you'd care to think. What they're trying to accomplish here isn't that different from what brought you here."

We shuffled our feet and cleared our throats. I thought about my objections to the missionaries, and about my own motives for coming here, about my confusion over who I was here to help. Was I using them to help myself? Was I any less a hypocrite?

Someone asked which held greater sway here – Christianity or the spirit world, and Barry thought about it. "I don't think you can quantify them," he said. "People here don't see a dichotomy in being Christians who fear sorcerers: animists and polytheists who worship Jesus."

He pointed out the window. "People out there farming *kau kau* in a plot cut from the side of a mountain, that's what they know. They see a jet airplane pass five miles overhead, and they have to keep that from upsetting their perceptions of the world around them. They have to reconcile the two. That," he said in summation, "takes magic."

I remembered our *wokabout* the day I arrived in the village, as Papa and Francis and I watched an airliner streak across the sky. I remembered their polite interest as I described my flight here, and I remembered their doubt. How could I help them make sense of that? It barely made sense to me.

Here, in the conference room at Kefamo, on the fulcrum between this world and the one I had left behind, I realized that as this new reality took more clarity and meaning for me, my world, my past, my life before, slid further away. I wondered where it went, and what would take its place.

When I think now about the discovery of Francis' goat, I can't separate it from what would happen a few days later. Even now, I can't tell if it was oddly coincidental or eerily significant. But I know that the woman had nothing to do with the events that followed. What I knew that day, as our discussion echoed from the painted walls and varnished floors, was that we were on to something important, something that cut to the heart of what we were doing here. I felt it again, this *presque vu*, this sense that I stood on the brink of an epiphany, a discovery that would help me to find what continued to elude me. But I still couldn't grasp it. The window had opened briefly, then closed again. I didn't know if it would ever come to me, or if I would even know if it did.

December 10, 1994 – Appointment in Samarra

The conversation about Francis' goat, and the superstitions around its death, lingered with me throughout the day and into the next. We talked about the goat's "fate," as if it were somehow predestined to meet that end, in that place, guided there by a destiny it could never have avoided.

It reminded me of an fable I had read in an English class, an ancient Middle Eastern tale retold in 1933 by W. Somerset Maugham. In it, a merchant in Baghdad sends his servant to shop in the market, but the servant soon returns, empty-handed and terrified. The merchant asks the servant why he failed to complete his errand, and the servant explains, "In the marketplace, I was pushed from behind by someone in the crowd, and I turned to find the face of Death, gazing upon me." The servant begs to borrow the master's horse, so he can leave and escape his fate. The merchant asks his servant where he will go, and the servant responds, "I'll go to Samarra, where Death will not find me." The merchant takes pity on the servant and gives him a horse, and the servant flees. Later that day, the merchant himself goes to town, and in the same market, he too finds Death amid the crowd. But the merchant does not flee. Instead, he approaches Death and asks, "Why did you threaten my servant when you saw him this morning?" Death replies, "I did not threaten him, I was merely surprised to find him in Baghdad. You see, I have an appointment with him tonight in Samarra."

Was it destiny that claimed Francis' goat? And was it destiny that would draw the woman to the people of my village that afternoon? She seemed to simply appear at the wedding, without reason or notice, and she returned with us to Mari-eka as if drawn there; an inescapable, unstoppable impulse. The first steps toward her own fate.

Mama had a cousin named Soti, who lived in a village a few miles to the west of ours, and she was getting married. My family and I, along with others from our village, got up early that Saturday to make our way to the ceremony. Aha-no walked with us, slowly but cheerfully plodding along the clay trail on his cracked and splayed bare feet.

We arrived to find a dozen warriors strutting across an open *singsing* ground, armed with stone axes, carved spears, bows and arrows. Sunlight glinted from their oiled skin as they smacked their weapons against their chests and slapped their feet on the packed earth, and their harsh tones and shrill calls pierced the smoky air.

Hundreds of friends and relatives, along with the face-painted warriors, had come for the ceremony. My family and I sat amid the tangled roots of a beech tree, and Papa described to me the ceremonial *bilas*, or decoration, that the people were wearing.

The warriors' faces were painted with bright reds and yellows, their skin smeared with oiled fat rendered from a pig. They draped the pelt of a bandicoot, a possum-like marsupial known in Pidgin as a *cuscus*, across their chests. They wore rattan armbands adorned with bones faded to a dull brown. "Those," Papa said, "are the bones of their ancestors, passed from the father to the son."

The warriors' cheeks and foreheads were coated in paint that cracked and flaked as it dried. The skin around their eyes was scarlet with dots of white and concentric blues, tiny azure orbs searching all directions at once, giving them a frenzied, maniacal look.

They wore brightly accented headdresses made from feathers of birds of paradise, jutting several feet from the crowns of their heads. Most of the feathers were black, flecked with blue, green, and turquoise, and the colors shone with a quicksilver hue. The feathers trembled with brutish grace as the warriors tossed their heads from side to side.

"The warriors from the husband's village are here to show that our daughter goes to a place with strong people," Papa explained, "who can look after her. Our warriors are to show that our daughter comes from strong people too, and she is worth fighting for."

He kept referring to Soti as 'our daughter,' though he wasn't her father, or even a blood relative. She was a *wantok*, "one talk," someone who shares a common language, a common heritage. *Wantoks* share everything. Accomplishments, failures, celebrations, tragedies; there were no individual experiences. I found a reassuring aptness to that sense of community and belonging, especially here in this imposing environment.

When the warriors stopped marching, the crowd cleared the *singsing* ground. "Now the ceremony begins," whispered Papa.

From the far side of the circle came an almost inhuman shriek, an absurd sound, like a performer overacting a role. The crowd separated, and warriors from the groom's village marched through. They walked in unison; knees high, and their weapons and feathers shuddering with each step. Forty warriors marched four abreast around the perimeter of the circle, eyes fixed before them.

At the head of the line marched an old man with shrunken skin, narrow limbs and knobby joints. His youth was long past, but he proudly wore the *bilas* of the warriors. He chanted steadily, and the others timed the cadence of their footsteps with his rhythm.

They marched for fifteen minutes, until another call came from our side, a jarring sound that again reverberated through the village. The crowd parted, and the warriors from Mari-eka stomped their way into the circle. They followed the same cadence, and now nearly 100 pairs of bare feet slapped out a steady, hypnotic thrum. Somewhere within the crowd, *kundu* drums began to sound.

Beneath a eucalyptus tree, Aha-no sat holding the hands of two children. He tucked his spindly legs beneath his grass skirt, and the mud applied to his face made his beard whiter even than usual. He fixed his eyes on the men in the circle and nodded slowly, absently chanting the cadence of their war cries. Bits of dried mud flaked from his beard and fell to his lap.

More warriors from the groom's village appeared, carrying poles twenty feet high. Dozens of *kina* notes were attached to the poles, the bills fluttering in the wind.

"A good bride price," Papa noted with satisfaction.

The transfer of the bride price is the apex of the ceremony. In the past, traditional bride price consisted of pigs and seashells, but modern commerce had replaced the shells with cash. The ritual presentation remained the same.

The tradition is tied as much to political and social relations as to finance. It isn't simply that the family of the groom is "purchasing" the bride; it's a symbolic offering of tribute, linking the villages to one another. It's also a form of compensation, acknowledging that the bride would be leaving her family to join her husband, and would therefore no longer be available to contribute to the well-being of her village.

Representatives of both sides engage in intricate negotiations to agree upon an acceptable exchange. Often, the entire village is involved in assembling the payment, reinforcing the community's stake in the marriage. But the woman herself seldom has any say, either in the negotiation of her bride price or in the choice of her husband. How he treats her is left essentially to his whim. Unfortunately, his whim often leads him to the violence that remains endemic to the Highlands.

After what seemed like hours, the drums fell silent and the warriors returned to their respective sides. The halt left a palpable stillness, somehow fuller than the cacophony that preceded it. In the vacuum of silence, the crowd cleared, and several men entered the *singsing* ground leading pigs with lengths of twine tied to a foreleg.

Papa gestured to the pigs with his chin. "Part of the bride price."

The men secured the leashes to stakes, and the pigs tugged at their restraints as elders from both villages examined them. One of the village elders wore a British safari cap and carried a rattan swagger stick, to go along with his grass skirt. They poked and prodded the pigs, scrutinizing their size and health. When the warriors returned to march again, the pigs remained tethered in the center, impatient with their leashes and frustrated with their inability to turn the hard clay with their snouts.

Finally, the bride and groom entered. They, too, wore traditional dress, their bare chests oiled, arms and legs wrapped in leaves and bones, smeared with mud. Their faces were painted, their eyes bordered with rings of scarlet and black, their foreheads yellow, dotted with white and blue. They wore more elaborate headdresses, with larger feathers and brighter bursts of color.

The bride, Mama's cousin, was about fifteen years old, with a round face shadowed with tribal tattoos. She was not as tall even as most Highland women, hence her name, Soti, "shorty." She wore a grass skirt, dyed orange and yellow, and a *bilum* slung across her forehead and draped over her back. Her bare breasts lay heavily on her oiled belly, and she walked slowly, full of solemnity, eyes cast downward. She looked nervous and shy, humbled by the reverence of the ceremony. She met her groom, a few years older than her, more than a foot taller, his eyes squinting narrowly against the sun, standing rigid and proud, and they walked the perimeter of the circle, between the two sets of chanting warriors.

The march of the bride and groom marked the end of the ceremony and led to the speeches. Leaders from both villages spoke, including Aha-no. Papa translated his *tok ples* into Pidgin for me.

He described the history between the villages, how this marriage would strengthen that heritage. He looked at the sky and pronounced it a fine day, a positive sign for the union. He spoke more but he grew tired, and his voice lost its strength. He coughed a rasping cough, and after a few minutes, he finished. Two of the warriors from Mari-eka helped him return to his spot in the shade beneath the eucalyptus.

Others spoke, but it was more than I could follow. The ceremony had gone all day, filled with ritual subtleties I didn't understand. We hadn't had eaten since morning, and daylight was waning. The speakers stood on the western edge of the village, and as the sun passed its zenith, it lowered directly behind them, gauging its rays relentlessly into the eyes of the listeners.

Following the speeches, the elders chose a few pigs for the feast. The crowd cleared, the pigs fidgeted, and warriors entered the *singsing* ground. One of them approached a female pig with brown spots, and she flicked her tied leg, trying to shake free of the leash as the warrior nocked an arrow. The muscles of his shoulders swam beneath the oil as he drew the bow, then released it, embedding it in an instant behind the pig's shoulder.

She staggered and fell as the leash pulled her leg from beneath her. Her squeals resounded like the earlier shrieks that cued the marching warriors. The pig tried to get up, her legs spasming, the arrow shaft jerking, as a thick pool of blood spread beneath her. The leash kept her stumbling in place, digging her face into the dirt again and again in a wretched, pathetic dance. She bled uncontrollably, and her panic made it worse. The other pigs jumped and stumbled over their leashes. Soon, she exhausted herself and collapsed, legs twitching, as she went through her final throes. Eventually, she lay still.

More pigs met the same fate, and several women butchered them, wrapping the chunks of meat in huge elephant ear leaves. A dozen chickens were slaughtered by machete and tossed to the women to be plucked, quartered and rolled into more leaves. The innards were tossed to a pack of dogs, who fought for them viciously. Bananas, *kau kau* and yams were all wrapped in the broad, green leaves.

The food was prepared *mumu*-style. The villagers had dug pits earlier in the day, and started fires nearby, placing large stones in the flames. The men used thick branches to remove the stones, now white-hot, and lower them into the earthen pits. Then they placed the wrapped food atop the stones and poured buckets of water over them, and it caused them to sizzle in the searing heat. Then, the pits were filled in with dirt, leaving small channels to allow the steam to escape.

I sat with my family as the food cooked. Aha-no joined us, taking my host brother Gilbert into his lap, and others came to see him. They welcomed me, shaking my hand, saying they had heard of me and knew I was doing well. We told pleasant stories. Papa's cousin Elvis arrived and was drunk, but he kept to himself. Everyone seemed jovial, and there would soon be plenty of food. Even Gilbert, who tended to cry whenever he looked at me, was chipper. Aha-no bounced him on his lap and held his hand. "*Brata bilong yu I stap,*" he whispered in Gilbert's ear, pointing at me, "Your brother is here."

When at last the *mumu* was ready, Papa handed me a leaf piled high with pork, including the choicest cut, a cube of gelatinous fat with a few thin striations of meat. The steam had melded the flavors together, imbuing them with an earthen, smoky taste. The meat was sodden and practically dissolved in my mouth. Liquefied fat dribbled into the whiskers on my chin, and bits of skin caught in my teeth. I forced a smile as the fat glistened around my mouth and dogs circled the crowd, awaiting cast-offs.

Darkness fell, and though much of the crowd remained, my family and I wished the newlyweds well and headed back for our village. As we walked, the sun slipped behind the mountains, though fragments of daylight remained to reflect from the clouds, offering enough illumination to make out the silhouettes of Francis and his children against the purpling sky. He was a giant compared to the little ones, who scurried around him in circles and eights, stumbling and laughing.

Another shape walked on the other side of Francis and carried one of his children, who rested his cheek on the top of her head. At first, I couldn't make out her face, but she was built much like Mama: wiry, pigeon-toed and barefoot, with narrow, spindly ankles.

Francis' wife had died a couple of years before, of an infection she developed after giving birth to their last child. The jovial Francis turned doleful at any mention of her, so I avoided the topic, but I had often wondered how difficult it must be for him to raise the kids on his own. Everyone in the village kept an eye on his family, and all families, but they were ultimately his kids.

I slowed my pace, knowing Mama and Papa would do the same to keep me nearby in the encroaching darkness. When I felt that Francis and the others were far enough away, I asked about the woman.

"Who is that?" I asked, gesturing toward her.

Papa reminded me that I had met her on our *wokabout* on my first day in the village. Then I remembered seeing her again, at the roadside market a few days later.

"Her mother was married to a man from our village," Mama said, "but he died before she was born. They moved back to her mama's village, and she grew up there. That is her place, but she wants to come to our village, to know about her papa's people."

"Is she," I didn't know how to phrase it, "with Francis?"

Mama coughed with laughter and embarrassment and slapped me in the arm.

"No!" she scolded. "She is not with Francis!"

I let it go. There was no more reason for me to dwell on it than on any of the other details I had observed on that or any other day. But that was the day that the woman's providence became entwined with, and dictated by, the people of my village.

I remember seeing her often over the next few weeks, but my memories remain unspecific; blurred snapshots from the recesses of my mind, distorted because I view them now through the lens of what would follow. I remember her expression as tense, pinched, as if irritated by some taste of bitterness, and I remember a deep and profound sadness in her eyes. At least, I think I remember those things. Or does my memory supplant reality with what I imagine?

What should become of the things we remember?

I remember her talking and laughing with the other women of our village, as if Mari-eka was her home. She would make herself comfortable there, washing the dishes and clothes alongside the other women, working in the gardens and sitting before the fires in the evenings. She came and went, sometimes staying for dinner and spending the night, other times returning to her own village. She spoke with the women in the same way they spoke with each other, with the same familiarity. It was as if she belonged there, had been destined all along to be there, propelled by fate to be in that very place, at that very time.

It made everything that happened afterward seem almost inevitable.

December 13, 1994 – Machines

As the days passed, my time in Mari-eka developed a routine, just as Barry had said it would. I became more accustomed to life in the Highlands, and I came to find deep satisfaction in sitting by the fire in the mornings, listening to the rooster's hoarse crow, drinking tea and eating hard crackers, or working in the garden, helping prepare for dinner, even passing the cantankerous Wilbur at the outskirts of the village every morning.

Papa prepared me for the endless procession of visitors who came to our village. He told me what their relationship was and how I should address them. He taught me how speak to strangers or landowners, how to express appreciation or respect. On hikes, when I stumbled along the trail, he was beside me to offer a hand. He watched me with a genuine paternalism, and I sought his approval.

Mama made sure I woke up on time and ate enough dinner. If it was cloudy, she insisted I carry my raincoat, and every night she meticulously washed every clump of mud from the soles of my boots so I wouldn't slip as I hiked up and down the mountain. She offered constant praise, with the boastful pride and unshaken faith a mother is meant to have for her child.

When I was a boy in Green Bay, my mom used to come to my youth league soccer games, even when my dad was my coach and they weren't getting along. I remember that my otherwise soft-spoken mother would let out a huge, heartfelt cheer every time I touched the ball, even though she didn't know or care what else was happening in the game. I still remember the tone of her voice racing across the field from the sideline as she celebrated as if I had just scored the deciding goal on an improbable, last-second trick shot. She seemed to think she had no choice but to cheer so loudly in order to drown out the collective roar which she imagined was sure to follow from my myriad other admirers, though there were none. I remember feeling an odd mixture of pride at having a fan, and the angst of an awkward teenager who didn't want to be singled out, believing I had done nothing worth cheering about.

My host mother in the village was no less enthusiastic in her praise, and I was no less self-conscious about it. She constantly assured me I was the finest volunteer in the entire Peace Corps; that I spoke the language better and had a deeper understanding of the culture than any other volunteer. She paid compliments to my height, my strength, my blue eyes and straight hair. She assured me I would find a strong, beautiful woman to marry, who would take care of me.

Yet there remained a distance in my relationship with her. I was coming to know the local men and boys through the conversations we had and the stories we told, but it seemed like whatever familiarity I had of the women of my village came only from what I knew about Highland women in general. The women of Mari-eka seldom spoke directly to me, and when they did, it was brief, awkward, and embarrassed. Their interaction with the other men of the village was only slightly more comfortable, but still often shaded by aloofness, and occasionally by intimidation.

Mama wouldn't have been more than a few years older than me; like most others in the village, she didn't know her exact age. But her years had been more wearying and demanding than any I could imagine, and while they lent her an undeniable authority, they also wore her down. Deep lines creased the edges of her eyes and the corners of her mouth. Her back stooped as if she'd carried too heavy a burden for too long.

There were times, rare instances, when I saw her as a girl, timid and eager, even child-like. When something caught her off-guard or embarrassed her, she would flinch and jerk her hand to her mouth to muffle an inadvertent laugh, a reflex that seemed to force her, in spite of herself, to allow a fleeting glimpse of her essence.

She seldom said anything about herself, and when I asked, she would turn her head to focus on Gilbert or some other task and deftly change the subject. The closest I had come to a personal insight about her was the story about day she chased away the woman Papa brought home to be his second wife, and it was Papa who told me about it, not her.

By indirect demonstration, she taught me the role Highland women play in their society – performing most of the labor, assuming most of the responsibility and reaping little of the reward. They worked in the gardens and carried the crops to sell at the markets while their children slept in *bilums* draped over their backs. They were caregivers to the men, but seldom their friends.

It seemed a lonely existence, yet Mama never seemed unhappy. Papa was good to her. He never hit her that I knew of, and I would come to learn that a husband who didn't beat his wife was a sad rarity in the Highlands, where domestic violence is not only accepted, it is considered the norm. A man who does not beat his wife runs the risk of being viewed by his peers as weak and even negligent, creating the pressure and expectation of inflicting violence purely for its own sake.

By contrast, Mama and Papa's relationship seemed safe and contented, and I found comfort in their company.

I liked being around Francis, too, because of his pure benevolence. He often drove me to Kefamo, and our conversations were light-hearted and filled with laughter. He had a natural gift for humor, a grasp of the ridiculous. He was skilled in the sideways look, the arched brow, the incredulous stare. I liked my *kandre*, my uncle, and his rowdy kids. He seemed to have figured out the difference between the things that mattered and those that didn't.

I also became friends with Tim and some of the younger guys in the village. They were closer to my age, and sometimes it was a relief to be with people who didn't care if I was sleeping or eating enough. They liked to hike, hunt, play rugby, flirt with girls, and talk about innocuous subjects of little consequence. The weight of the world had not yet dulled them. They avoided unpleasantness and seriousness– because those things aren't fun.

I saw Aha-no almost every day. He wanted constant appraisals of my progress. He often joined us for dinner, and occasionally he hiked with us, though he could seldom go far. At times, when he could tell I was feeling homesick, he would sit beside me on one of the stones at the edge of the hearth and speak to me in simple phrases about his youth; the war, the *kiaps*, the encroachment of the outside world and the upheaval it brought. He told mythical, dreamlike tales of an era and a place that no longer existed except in his own memory. He had never been in an airplane, never seen a car until he had married his wife, never had an electric light. He didn't know how machines worked, but he understood how people used them to control each other.

We talked about the "cargo cults" that proliferated during his childhood. As World War II raged in the South Pacific, the Allies dropped food and equipment from airplanes to supply their soldiers. Villagers who witnessed these drops believed the whites had used witchcraft to summon cargo, which took on a spiritual significance for them. They grew to worship the crates of food and materiel strewn across their lands and the machines that delivered them. And they came to fear the magic of the whites. Highlanders saved empty cans and other trash discarded by the whites, believing them to be totems of their magic. Cargo became a religion.

Aha-no described the cults with bemusement. Technology never awed him. Instead, he had recognized from the beginning how it could be used to subdue his way of life, and that of his people. Machines were not to be trusted.

Along with the spread of the cargo cults came the missionaries, canvassing the Highlands for fresh converts. The two sometimes struggled for supremacy in a single village. In a sense, Aha-no saw Western religion as another machine, like the phonograph player brought by Leahy expedition, trapping men's souls. It was just a trick, not real magic.

As a symbol of his resistance, he shunned the introduced modesty of Western clothing and continued to walk about the village in his *tanget* leaf skirt. He was a happy relic, and he seemed to share my own misgivings about the notion of the outside world "developing" or "saving" the people here.

The people of the Highlands didn't have the cushion of multiple generations in which to grow accustomed to the philosophies of modern technology. For them, it happened almost in an instant, in less than a generation. And so the neuroses that affect us all, as our machinery and technology dramatically changes the world around us and supersedes what we consider to be our

99

humanity, our connection to others and the planet, impacted the Papua New Guineans so much more acutely. Simply because, in an instant, the way they viewed the world was turned upside down and inside out, and they were more noticeably forced to live at odds with themselves.

But not Aha-no. This frail little man remained in complete harmony with himself and his surroundings. Above all, he was a realist. He knew the changes and upheaval brought upon his society by the missionaries and the colonials were inevitable. Born into a society that didn't use the wheel, there were now fax machines whirring along with the cicadas not fifteen miles from his village. He had absorbed these changes with grace and aplomb, and Barry was right, that did take a little magic. But Aha-no understood the roles played by the machinery of religion and of change. He held fast before them and stood as an example for his people as they struggled to do the same.

Maybe that was why he took to me the way he did. Maybe he recognized even better than I did that my role was to do something similar; to help ease that transition. To stand beside him and his people and to reassure them as they journeyed into a world that was new, unfamiliar, sometimes unfriendly, but ultimately unavoidable. I had won the honor of his trust, and he had welcomed and embraced me. His acceptance was immediate, complete– and humbling.

I came home to Mari-eka one afternoon to find Francis and some others peering beneath the raised hood of his truck with the same admixture of enchantment and boredom they wore when watching an animal being slaughtered for a *mumu*. Francis nodded as I arrived, but then he returned his attention to the machine, absorbed with manhandling its decayed components.

"Battery," he said, his voice echoing from the raised hood, "*bagarap.*"

Bagarap was another introduced word. When something was broken, the Australians would say it was 'buggered up,' and as things were often broken in the jungles of the South Pacific, they found a lot of use for the phrase, so it made its way into the lexicon of Pidgin.

"Here, you see?" Francis pointed to the battery. "Here is where it is buggered." The positive and negative terminals had both broken off; leaving nowhere to attach the cables.

"You need a new one," I said, but Francis shook his head.

"We'll fix it," he responded, still staring at the battery.

I raised an eyebrow and asked, "You can fix that?"

He turned to Tim and the others and spoke to them in *tok ples*. Having received their instructions, they raced back to the village, while Francis removed the battery from its casing and lugged it toward the *singsing* ground.

A fire burned in the center of the village, and we situated ourselves around it. Papa appeared in the doorway of our hut and whistled for Francis, then tossed him an empty mackerel tin and ducked back inside. One of Francis' children brought a length of lead solder and handed it to Francis. He set the solder in the empty can and then placed them into the fire. Flames pirouetted and caressed the sides of the tin, blackening them with carbon, and the solder melted into a thick, silvery liquid, pooling at the bottom of the fish can.

Tim arrived carrying several stalks of bamboo, and Papa reemerged from our hut with his machete. He took the bamboo from Tim and cut each stalk to a length of a couple of inches. Each worked without speaking, seeming to know what was expected of him, cutting bamboo, tending the fire, or scraping away the corrosion on the surface of the battery.

Tim positioned the bamboo stalks over the terminal points and Francis poured liquid solder into the mold. They repeated the process on the other side, then waited to allow it to cool. Everyone lapsed into idle chatter, no one looking at anyone else, staring instead at the dusty battery. We talked about people we knew, places we'd been. They asked me questions about my home and my family in the States, old friends, girls; questions they'd asked and I'd answered many times before, but it didn't matter. We were only *storying*, covering ground that had by now become familiar. Though our eyes never left it, we spoke of anything but the battery until the terminals cooled and Francis pried the bamboo away.

As the sun began retreating toward the end of a languid day, a blazing palette of color streaked across the evening sky, an exquisite backdrop against which the battered truck with its raised hood appeared stark and frail in its modernity. Francis and the others were shadows and silhouettes as the clamor of the village dwindled, and the voices of Francis and his crew became distinct and soulful against the relative silence; disembodied tones floating from the pale dimness. The sounds of tools clattering against the engine block, or of corroded nuts squealing against their bolts, were the only signifiers of work being done. The vehicle appeared serene, accepting, unmoved by the efforts made toward its preservation.

Eventually, Francis replaced the battery in its housing and connected the cables. The hood remained raised, and he climbed into the driver's seat. I backed away and searched through the fading light for the spot where I estimated the soldered posts would be. Francis turned the key, and current hummed through the ersatz terminals. Sparks leapt from the posts, more noticeable in the early dusk, but then they subsided, and the engine turned, coughed, and settled into a healthy idle. I stood in my spot, amazed.

One of the boys lowered the hood, Francis eased the truck into gear, and he drove triumphantly past the village gate. A few boys hopped into the back and hung on to each other's shirts as they headed down the trail, singing and laughing.

I watched them go, in dumbfounded awe of their ingenuity in crafting this makeshift contraption, repairing a car battery using nothing but a machete, a few pieces of bamboo, a few ounces of solder and a dented, tin can crucible.

And as I watched the taillights dissolve into a faint and smoky dusk that would soon give way to the nothingness of night, a breeze sieved through the village, carrying the perfume of orchids and night-blooming cereus and slowly dispersing the remaining heat of the day. The sounds of the truck faded, morphing into the pulsing hymn of insects and calls of frogmouths and nightjars. Standing alone to the side of the village, I lapsed into a grin of child-like wonderment, my face warmed by a waning amber glow that emanated from beneath the clouds.

I began to feel a curious and strangely complacent sense that the sublime glory of that sunset signaled not just the end of this day, but the end of all days; the end of all the world. There was a finality to the auburn glow of the night sky, a triumphant, almost symphonic closing, and I just couldn't imagine anything could follow such an apt conclusion.

I felt a sense, a revelation, that the ground beneath me was a living thing, pulsing, trembling, like a cat twitching its tail. It felt as if a shiver ran across the spine of the mountain as it turned to situate itself, and I had the dizzying sense I was falling, dropping away from the edge of the world, lost in the enormity of all that surrounded me.

The slow withdrawal of daylight had been resolute and irrevocable, but somehow, in the splendor and ease of evening, in the supremacy of the coming darkness, the implicitness of its silence, I felt no sadness, only peace. It was right, it was true, and it was perfect.

I told myself this wasn't actually the end of days, suddenly believing with the faith of a convert that another day would follow this one. But someday, when the end does come, I imagined this was how it would happen. Not as a cataclysm or an apocalypse, but instead as a slow exhalation, a gentle winding down, as the earth lays itself to rest in simple, satisfied contentment.

T.S. Eliot wrote, "This is the way the world ends, not with a bang but a whimper." And I thought, maybe that wouldn't be so bad.

December 16, 1994 – Twilight

"How old are you?" I asked Aha-no as he grasped a few grains of rice between curled, trembling fingers, lifted his hand and opened his mouth to drop the clump through the gaps between his teeth.

It was just the two of us at dinner that night. Mama and Papa had gone to visit an ill relative and thought it might be better if I stayed behind. The presence of a stranger, especially a white man, might be too exhilarating for someone in their relative's condition. Aha-no had come to keep me company, and now he looked at me over the cooking fire and arched his brow.

"Eh?" he whispered.

"How old?" I gestured through trailing wisps of smoke. "How many years?"

I had asked the question before and never found a satisfactory answer. I don't know why I was preoccupied with his age. I suppose it was some sociological instinct to define and categorize him, attach to him some quantifiable label, as if it might help me to more easily understand, and assess, his significance and his value.

He chuckled. "*Lapun*," he said. "Old."

I persisted. "How many years?" I asked.

He shrugged his bony shoulders. He didn't know.

His earliest memories were of piston-engine fighter planes droning overhead during the war, more than fifty years ago. The world had changed in the years that followed, and Aha-no had grown to an old age. He must have been in his sixties when I came to his village, and in the Highlands, that qualified him as more than old– he was ancient. And he looked it, from the deep lines that crept across his ashen face, the sagging flesh that hung from his jaw, as if he were melting before the fire, like a candle flickering on an altar.

I tried to envision the child he must have been, running barefoot over the clay paths that carved his village from the rainforest. In a way, I thought I could see, or at least imagine, the boy that hid behind his tired eyes, though that child was little more than a dim flicker beneath the milky cataracts of the man who sat across from me now. Yet it was clear he could still speak to that boy, about all that had transpired since.

He came of age at a crucial time in the collective experience of his culture. He would have been born around 1930, the same year the Leahys first entered the Goroka Valley. The world into which he had been born, in which nothing existed beyond the perimeters of tribe and family, home and forest, disappeared with his childhood. Yet his instincts and his doggedness had kept him going, well past the life expectancy of most Highlanders, beyond man's measure of time.

Within the span of a few short years, the people of the Highlands were inundated with a millennium of technological and social evolution: electricity, telephones, cars, airplanes, computers, God, and gold. When the whites stumbled upon the Highlands, the tribes still fought one another with spears and arrows; a mere decade later, the atomic age had dawned.

All this change had been thrust upon the inhabitants of the Highlands within a single lifetime – his lifetime. The source of his wisdom was that he understood the journey his people had taken over the course of those years. None of it surprised him, none of it threw him. Somehow, it all made sense to him.

He smiled at me across the fire and repeated, "*Lapun,*" and I could only smile back.

The literary tradition of our culture instills in us an instinctive expectation of how change comes. The way we perceive the narrative arc of our stories, from books to music to movies, even to our own memory, impresses upon us a powerful sense of anticipation. Words foreshadow, our pulses quicken, and the teller of the tale, as in this tale, pauses and gives us a moment to draw a breath.

This moment, pregnant with what is to come, foretells the approach of transformation, and we obediently await its arrival. In this interlude, we see ourselves on the precipice of change, we envision how it will affect us, and we steady ourselves for what must come next.

But in reality, when change comes and the epiphany arrives, we are rarely afforded the luxury of foresight. We don't see it coming. There is no pause. What arrives is unanticipated, chaotic, an unwelcome intrusion into the predictability and safety of ubiquitous routine, and we are unprepared. All we can do is snap to, awaken, blink away the stupor of the mundane and find that the moment has arrived; it is happening now.

Whether we stand and watch or become a participant is up to us. But the transformation will take place, with or without us.

In the early morning hours of December 19, 1994, change came to the little village of Mari-eka.

December 18–19, 1994 – Darkness

I found myself jarred from sleep by the sound of someone shuffling frantically around the inside of our hut. The kerosene lantern cast a feeble glow against the thatched bamboo wall, where a shadow danced. I struggled into consciousness and angled my watch toward the lamp's weak light. My heart began to pound against my chest. Something was wrong. They say no one wakes you up at 3:00 in the morning with good news. A heavy rain slapped against the roof. I tried to focus on the figure.

"Papa?" I said, and he turned to me, his face twisted in anguish and shadow.

"Nipi'e," he stammered, "I need your torch." He meant the small flashlight I kept in my duffel bag.

I sat up and rubbed my eyes. "*Em wanem*?" I asked. "What is it?"

"Aha-no," he said, stammering in short, shallow breaths. "*Em dai.*"

He died.

I tried to focus on Papa. "What?"

"Nipi'e, please. I need your torch."

I pulled back the mosquito net, grasped the flashlight and handed it to Papa. He snatched it and said, "Now go back to sleep."

"Wait," I said, struggling out of my sleeping bag. "I'll go with you."

"Nipi'e," he held up a hand. "You have to get up soon. Stay here."

"Papa, please," I insisted. "I want to go."

He paused and then nodded, and I pulled on my boots and my raincoat and we bolted through the door, amid the chorus of rain falling on the dark and empty *singsing* ground. Still warm from sleep, the shock of the cold rain jolted me into consciousness, and I began to shiver uncontrollably.

Papa raced ahead of me, and I kept on his heels. We climbed the gate, and I watched the beam of the flashlight swing a crazy loop through the darkness ahead. It illuminated almost nothing, but I'd been over this trail so many times, I knew exactly where we were going.

As we came to the hill that led to Aha-no's hut, we leapt the drainage ditch along the side of the trail and scrambled through the undergrowth. A stalk of wet *kunai* grass slid across my cheek and sliced the skin beneath my eye.

Atop the plateau, we found Francis and some others from the village. Someone had brought a kerosene lamp, this one a pressure lantern, and it cast a strong, dazzling light. They had draped a raincoat over the lantern to keep it dry, and it cast a long shadow and emitted an eerie hiss as the kerosene vaporized in the flue.

Aha-no lay in the mud on his side, his legs splayed as if trying to run. His mouth and eyes were open, and raindrops slapped at his grizzled beard, making the whiskers flinch as if the flesh at their roots were still alive and recoiling from the affront. I felt a powerless indignation as the elements continued to assault the lifeless old man. The same rain that had fallen steadily and predictably throughout his life in these Highlands continued to descend without pause around the frailty of his remains, as we gazed on helplessly.

We crouched around him, and no one moved or spoke. In the distance, through black sheets of rain, several women unleashed sustained cries of sorrow. I looked toward the village, but saw only darkness, blanketing the wraithlike voices.

"Go now," Papa instructed me. "We will take care of him."

"I want to stay," I said, and I turned to face him through the increasing intensity of the rain driving between us. I found something distant and unexpected in his expression. There was grief there, but something else too; a sense of determined resolve, as if there were something remaining, something he had to do.

The old man was gone and couldn't be brought back – what was there aside from sadness?

"Go home," Papa repeated, and his expression left no room for argument. I looked to Francis, but he only nodded, his eyes fixed on the old man. Papa offered me the flashlight, but I shook my head.

People express sorrow in different ways, and cultures do, too. The people of my village thought it best that I go, and I had to accept that. As much as I wanted to be there for them in the moment of their loss, a loss I felt I shared with them, I didn't know where I fit in this grief. For the people of the village, mourning was an active, physical expression. They wailed and shouted in their sorrow, as if the pure force of their lungs might somehow expel the pain in their chests. They swayed and moved, flinging their hands at their sides, and slapping their breastbones, bemoaning with hoarse voices the fate of the old man. Their anguish was desperate, almost violent, but despite their overt articulations, there was an intimacy in their anguish that made me feel I couldn't join them. I wouldn't have known how.

I had never lost anyone close to me. A few distant relatives had died during my childhood, but they were little more than names and faces, polite greetings, pats on the head. And Green Bay was a stoic, aloof place where the most overt expressions of emotion tended to hinge on the outcome of football games. When I was fifteen, a school classmate was murdered in a nearby field, and for a few weeks it was all anyone could talk about. But we never actually said a word to each other about how we felt about it. The school made counselors available for those students who felt they needed to process the complex emotions associated with the violence, the tragedy and the loss, but as far as we knew, none of us kids took them up on their offer. We wouldn't have had any idea how. We repressed our emotion, swallowed it, pushed it down and pretended it wasn't there.

I wasn't going to pretend the sadness of Aha-no's death wasn't there, but I didn't know how to express it to the people of my village, and they didn't seem to want me to. After a final look at the old man, I left, and within moments, I had returned to our hut and began stripping off my soaked clothes. Mama was gone, and, with her, Gilbert. I was alone. I dried myself with my camp towel, moldy from its time in these gray and clouded mountains, and I ducked beneath my mosquito net, my skin cold and clammy. Drawing my sleeping bag around me, I shivered and knew I wouldn't sleep. I tossed and turned, trying to settle myself; to calm my mind and find some order there. Shock had not yet turned to the simple sadness of acceptance.

For the rest of the night, I faded into and out of a light sleep, fitful and restless. Occasionally, I realized I was awake, my eyes open and staring into the dull grayness of the hut. A moth flitted across my eyelid and I realized I had forgotten to lower my mosquito net or douse the hurricane lamp. I couldn't find the energy to reach either of them. Instead, I lay motionless, and I waited for the night to pass.

December 19, 1994 – Sorrow

Dawn arrived, and with it came the weeping of the villagers, their cries becoming louder, more insistent, adopting a tone of increasing anguish. Blackness dissolved to paler gray, enhanced by a lambent glow a few feet from me as the hurricane lamp, which had burned all night, withered through its final dregs of kerosene. The distant sounds of a woman's cry threaded through my nascent consciousness. The cicadas droned, but Francis' children were silent.

As much as I wanted to believe the previous night had been a bad dream; there hadn't been enough of a break between night and day to give reason to wonder. There had only been the sputtering hurricane lamp, the upturned mosquito net, the silence of death broken by the sound of whimpering, which had removed me from the refuge of distant, wakeful dreams.

The crying of one woman in particular had a strange edge to it, as if it were not just escaping her throat of its own accord but were instead being forced out and flung across the village. The sound unnerved me, and I got up and pulled on a shirt from the floor; the same one I had worn a few hours before, still wet from the rain.

Mama and Papa hadn't returned, and for a moment the village sat in tranquil quietude until it was broken again by the anguished woman's crying, which I realized was coming from the hut immediately beside ours, which had previously been used for storage. I stood still for a moment, seeking meaning in the different tone of her cry, but silence returned to engulf the village.

A dismal, bruised sky hung low, morning sunlight diffused almost to nothingness by thick haze. Gray mist draped the village in a funerary shroud, sorrowful and unmoving. Through it, I found Mama and Papa, along with several others, huddled before a fire. Their faces looked bloodless. I felt a lump welling in my throat.

"*Sori tumas,*" I said, my voice jarring the silence. "I am very sorry."

Papa nodded; his face wan. Mama pressed her fingers to her eyes, and tears rolled across the tattoos on her cheeks. Then, she removed her hands and fixed her bloodshot eyes on mine. "It is time for you to go to your school," she managed to say.

I shook my head. "I won't go today," I said. "I'll stay here."

"No," Papa interjected. "You will go." The voice was resolute, as it had been a few hours earlier when he had sent me home. Again, I didn't argue.

The silence, enshrined in the heavy fog, was again broken by the wailing voice, and I turned toward the sound. There were no fires burning within any of the empty huts. Everyone was here, except the source of that voice, crying so desperately.

Something aside from pure sadness propelled that sound, an undeniable sense of urgency and need. "*Em husat?*" I asked. "Who is that?"

No one answered, but Papa put his hand on my arm. "Nipi'e," he said to me, looking plaintively into my eyes, "it is time for you to go."

I understood they wanted to make sure I got to training; that I didn't fall behind or get into trouble. But I sensed their insistence this morning was motivated by more than simple concern.

They didn't want me there.

Barry had told us no matter what, there would be times we would not be a part of what was happening around us. I accepted that – they had a right to expect certain things to be kept distinct and sacred. Maybe mourning the loss of a family member was such a deeply cultural expression, so steeped in tradition, that they needed to be alone.

Mama stood with me. "Nipi'e, it's cold," she said, gently raising the hood of my raincoat to cover my head. "Be careful," she added.

"I will," I promised, consumed by my helplessness.

I was filled with regret as I abandoned my family, but I knew they wanted me to go.

I couldn't tell where I belonged.

I climbed the gate and began walking along the path. The ornery pig Wilbur, who so frequently blocked my path, was nowhere to be seen this morning, as though even he sensed the heaviness in the air. Ahead, through the mist, I recognized Elvis in his ski coat, staggering up the path. Drawing nearer, he lifted an arm and waved, then stumbled on a stone outcrop and cursed.

"Nipi'e!" he called in a dull voice.

He approached and clapped an unwelcome hand on my shoulder. "You know about Aha-no?" he said. His breath reeked of the sickening sweet smell of the cheap Buttercup rum sold in the trade stores.

I nodded. "I saw him last night."

There wasn't much to say, and I had turned to move on when Elvis mumbled, "*Bai mipela kilim i dai!*" I kept moving away, thinking I'd misunderstood– "We're going to kill them." But then I stopped and turned to Elvis.

"What?" I asked.

"She did this." He flung his arm toward our village, a gesture of grandiose futility against a clouded, tumultuous sky. "And she will die for it."

I stared at him. "Who?" I asked.

He drew a breath, as if bracing his patience to speak to an overly curious child. "Last night, the witch came for Aha-no. She took his heart. She killed him."

Immediately, I regretted stopping to listen to this insanity. But I also remembered our recent discussions about perceptions of the spirit world, how strong an influence it held here. I remembered Papa hurrying to deliver us back to the village before dark, when the spirits claimed the night. I remembered the morning I met Barry. "Spirits, ancestors, sorcerers," he'd said. "People here believe they're involved with even the simplest occurrences. Sickness, accidents, crops, weather, it's all controlled by the spirits. No one can avoid it." And I remembered Francis' goat, its chest sliced open, its insides spilled onto the ground, exposing its secrets to the villagers' chagrin and my bewilderment.

Elvis went on. "We went to get her, the witch. We found her together with a woman, so we took them both. And we will punish the one who is responsible."

Dread seeped through me. There were two women in the hut. Theirs were the voices I had heard crying.

"Who are they?"

Elvis shrugged, swayed, and almost fell. "That woman," he said, "who followed us home from the marriage ceremony for Soti. And another. I don't know. We took them both," he said again.

I thought back to the day the woman had accompanied us home from the wedding. In the days since, she had appeared regularly in the village, but my only interaction with her stemmed from her typical curiosity about the oddity of my white skin. I had seen her with the other women, taking the washing to the stream, or on their way to the gardens, her thin mouth stretched into a haunted smile.

But *was* her smile haunted, even then? Was it doomed? Did she somehow know?

What should become of the things we remember?

Elvis lurched up the path toward the village, and I stood for a moment, wondering what to do. I knew there had been something different in the voices coming from that hut; something simpler and more immediate than sadness. Now I knew what it was.

They were afraid.

I had to talk to my family. Aha-no hadn't died because of witchcraft; he had died because he was old. He had already outlived most Highlanders, and he had been frail for years. His heart finally gave out. I could explain that to them. I could make them understand.

But there had been a determination in Papa unlike anything I had seen in him before. I knew that what I was considering was unprecedented in my relationship with my family. Everything I had done in that village up to that point had been at their invitation. This was different. I would be offering a perspective no one wanted to hear, advice for which no one asked. My input wouldn't be welcomed or appreciated.

I watched the gaudy jacket bob up and down as Elvis stumbled along the path and dissolved into the drifting fog. I turned again and headed down the mountain, consoling myself with the notion that he was drunk and babbling. He'd probably made it up.

I hoped the walk would clear my head. Too many things were distracting me. Aha-no had died, and I still needed to absorb that. The silence should have aided my thoughts. No one greeted me from the huts I passed on the trail or hailed me from the surrounding hills. By now, everyone would know what had happened, and I could feel the sense of solemnity and loss, as palpable as the heavy mist. Still, my head spun.

An hour later, I crossed the manicured grass of Kefamo's placid lawn. Before the conference room, I kicked off my mud-caked boots. A few of the other volunteers were inside, reading or catching some sleep. Dave, who had shared that first ride into Kefamo with me, reclined on the couch wearing a knitted *bilum* cap like Sonny's, which his host family had made for him. He was writing a letter.

"Seen Barry?" I asked.

He arched his eyebrows.

"Jesus," he said. "You look like shit." I didn't respond, and he gestured toward the south end of Kefamo. "He's in the library."

I headed in that direction.

"Hey," he called after me, and I turned back. "I heard about the old man." It didn't surprise me to find that the news had already spread through the other villages. "Did you know him well?"

"I guess so," I said, my mind blank. "I don't know."

"I'm sorry," Dave offered.

"Yeah," I said dumbly. "Me, too." I turned and headed toward the library.

I found Barry gazing intently at a large book splayed across a coffee table, showing photographs of the Papua New Guinean rainforests. I had thumbed through the same book a dozen times. Its cover had a picture of a narrow and steep mountain trail amid a tropical downpour: vivid, rich, living color distorted by an opaque curtain of voluminous rain, so thick and intense you could almost hear its roar just from the photo. It was a stunning portrait of the awesome and unrelenting supremacy of nature, a potent emblem of our powerlessness against it.

I crossed the library floor and dropped, heavily, into the chair facing

Barry's. He closed the book with gentle reverence, like a priest closing a bible after the recitation of a poignant passage.

"Morning." His tone was traced in sympathy. He paused, then said, "I heard."

"What did you hear?" I asked.

He exhaled slowly. "About the old man," he said. "And I'm sorry. He was special. He was one of the reasons we wanted to place someone in that village."

Neither of us knew what to add.

"Well," I told him, "there's more."

He pushed up his glasses to match his raised eyebrows. "Oh?"

"Have you heard anything about a couple of women locked in a hut?"

His eyebrows dropped and his shoulders slumped, and I watched his expression fall.

"No," he finally said.

"I don't know what's happening. For all I know, it's bullshit." Then I relayed the story, describing what Elvis had told me.

Barry listened without interruption, nodding periodically as I relayed everything, beginning with the night before and ending with Elvis' resolve that they were going to kill the women.

"They're not going to do this, are they?" I was almost pleading now.

He looked across the table at me. "It's happened before."

"What do I do?" I asked.

"What do you want to do?"

"I was hoping you'd tell me," I requested, but he didn't respond. "I don't even know if this is real," I said. "Elvis was drunk, and he's kind of the village idiot. Maybe it was just the booze talking, you know?"

"You said you heard voices coming from the hut," he reminded me.

"But that doesn't mean they're gonna kill them, does it? Maybe they just want to scare them."

But Barry shook his head. "It doesn't work that way…"

"I don't think they'd do something like that," I interrupted. "I know these people." But I stopped myself. I wanted to believe that, but in truth I had only been there a few weeks. Did I know them?

Barry said nothing, just watched me. Uncomfortable, I looked at my watch.

"Let's wait a little," I said. "I'll go back this afternoon and see what's going on." Stalling, while I hoped a better outcome would present itself.

Barry stood, and I made to follow him. "You don't look like you slept much." He pointed to the couch. "Why don't you try to get some rest, ah? We'll talk more later."

He closed the door behind him, and I curled on my side on the couch and closed my eyes. I dozed on and off for an hour, but then I gave up and joined the others for language lessons.

A few hours later, at lunchtime, Barry and I sat at a table, an untouched plate of food front of me, while Barry gripped the handle of a cup of tea. Today was a typical meal at Kefamo– frenzied and chaotic, with the competitive urgency of a high school football game. The dining room was a cacophony of sound and motion, shouts and insults only vaguely muffled by chewing food and swilling cordial.

Barry sat and observed, but ate nothing. He was fasting – something he told us he had been doing intermittently for years – which gave him an air of spiritual discipline and asceticism, made him seem like a sage.

"You want to go up and talk sense into them, right?" he asked, and then he shook his head. "It wouldn't matter. They'd be convinced you're the one who doesn't understand, and let's face it, you don't. You can't relate to this. This is a symbolic action, a statement they feel compelled by thousands of years of history to make, regardless of how they feel about it. It's an obligation. Whatever they do, it won't be because they will get any relief from it. It's what they believe they're *supposed* to do."

I realized Barry had no doubt they were going to do it. I had seen him work his way to that conclusion. Over the course of the conversation he had spoken first of the possibility, then the likelihood, then the certainty. He knew from the start where this was going, and he was trying to ease me into it.

But I wasn't prepared to accept it. I couldn't envision my family doing something like this. It was all too fast; Aha-no had only died a few hours before. I convinced myself they would realize that what they were doing was wrong. They would free those women so they could focus on grieving their loss.

117

Everything would be okay.

I crossed the bridge outside my village that evening beneath a sun vanishing into sedimentary oranges and pinks, dusted with pale clouds that faded to a smoky gray. The majesty of the evening made it impossible for me to believe there could be anything wrong in the world, and I stood for a while and stared, just breathing. But the moment was ebbing with the daylight, and despite my need to hold it a little longer, the sun continued to fade into the distant mountains, bleeding itself dry.

I stopped when I saw Francis sitting at the edge of the ravine, on the ledge that overlooked the waterfall where the kids had watched me wash. He too was absorbed by the dying light. He held a stubby of SP beer tucked between his knees and a stalk of *kunai* clenched in his teeth. I walked down the trail to sit beside him.

"*Apinun, kandre,*" I said. "Hello, uncle."

He turned to me and he offered an unconvincing smile. "Nipi'e," he said, and he offered a drink of his tepid beer. "Your people know what is happening?" he asked, gazing across the ravine.

I nodded and took a drink, then returned the stubby to him, and he drank. He wiped his beard, offered me the bottle again and nodded his head with certainty.

"We thought you weren't coming back," he said.

"I'm here," I said, to reassure myself as much as Francis.

Because in truth, I had thought about leaving. Nothing would have been easier. I had done it many times before. Since I was a kid, when things got difficult, complicated, serious, I left. It had become habit. I left Green Bay, I left our church, I left my family. I had left girlfriends, friendships, soccer teams. I could always be counted on to take the easier way out. Why not here? Why not now? If ever I could be excused for running away, allowing it to be someone else's worry, this was the time. I wouldn't have to second guess the decision, wouldn't have to grapple with the guilt of abandoning them. They wouldn't even have been surprised. They hadn't expected me to come back, anyway.

Francis clapped his hand on my shoulder and I nearly spilled what was left of the beer. "I'm happy to see you," he said. I returned the bottle to him, and he finished it.

"*Kandre*," I said. "What will happen to those women?"

His smile faded, and he fidgeted with the bottle, then hefted it and sent it spinning over the ledge into the abyss. We never heard it land. He released a slow, heavy sigh.

"*No save*," he said, "I don't know." I waited for something more, but he only pulled at his beard and stared across the ravine. Together, we watched the final fragments of daylight retreat into the punishing western sky.

"I don't want them to die," I finally told Francis.

"It's time for you to go," he responded, his voice dull. "Your Mama will worry."

The buzzing of flies and the trill of the cicadas were giving way to the more rhythmic and lyrical chirping of crickets. As I came into the village, I found none of the usual activity there: no one did the wash or worked in the gardens. The *singsing* ground sat empty and forlorn. The children didn't chase or call to each other. All was sedate, with almost no movement. The hut in which the women were locked sat quiet and still, but as I approached, I heard a hushed voice, like the rasping of dried corn stalks, and another answered it.

I entered our hut to find Papa crouched before the fire, preparing dinner. He nodded as I stepped through the door, but I could almost feel his apprehension. From the edge of the fire, I watched him cook.

Dinner was quiet, too; the silence occasionally punctuated by muffled sounds next door. When I could no longer stand it, I asked, "What's going to happen to them?"

He looked up at me from the fire. "We haven't decided," he said.

"What do you think they did?"

He sat back on his hams and studied me. "Those women are *sanguma meri*. A *sanguma meri* will choose someone, get close to him, make this person know her and trust her, as this woman did with us. She came here, stayed with us, ate our food, took our kindness. We trusted her because we are good people. We wanted to help her. Aha-no trusted her, and he believed she needed our help. She was alone."

119

He stopped, pulled a pan from the fire, and tossed it to the side. "And no one should be alone."

He was telling me more than he had seemed willing this morning. "But what did they do?" I asked.

"She waited until she found Aha-no alone," he said. "She reached into his chest, and she took out his heart. Then she breathed her air into him, so he would live long enough for her to leave this place. When the air was gone, he died."

I shook my head, exasperated. "Papa, that's…"

"No," he said suddenly. "No more talk about this. We have a responsibility to Aha-no. Because of these women, he is not finished. We cannot leave it this way. We must finish it. We will do what we can for him." His voice was final. He had turned back to his cooking. "We will do what we must for Aha-no," was all he had to say.

After we ate, a voice called from the distance through the night air. Papa shouted in return and stood. He glanced at me. "You are tired, and you should sleep. It's no good if you get sick." Then he crept through the door and disappeared into the darkness.

Mama rounded the edge of the fire and took my bowl from me. Though I'd hardly touched the food, she had no reproach for me on this night.

"Mama," I began. "This…" I searched for the words but failed to find them. I gestured in the direction of the hut next door. "This is wrong."

She leaned toward me and brushed the hair away from my forehead, a gesture of exquisite maternal grace, and she smiled a tiny smile. "Your Papa is right," she told me. "You are tired. You need to sleep." With that, she scooped up Gilbert, and carried the dishes out to wash them in the stream, leaving me alone again.

That night passed as the one before it had. I drifted into and out of awareness, but never really slept. I revisited my thoughts and my fears, tried to convince myself this couldn't happen.

I thought of what I said to Barry; that I knew these people, and they wouldn't do something like this. Maybe it happened in other villages, maybe it was sadly common in these islands, maybe there are even places where a different framework of morality does exist, and the notions of right and wrong are not so simple as to be encapsulated into absolutes. But not here. Not these people, not the ones who slept each night so soundly, so peacefully, just a few feet from me.

They're better than that. They're better than me.

I could go and open the door to the hut, I thought. Even if it was padlocked, it wouldn't take much to knock down one of the walls. The flimsy woven bamboo would come down easily. But there were villagers there, watching the hut, and they would catch the tired and frightened women. Maybe I should call out to the women; reassure them that it would be all right. But I knew, and they would know, too, that there was no basis for me to say it. I was no more certain of it than they were. In the end, I lay frozen, immobilized by indecision, sleepless once again. Waiting.

Their voices refused to be ignored.

December 20, 1994 – Dilemmas

The women in the hut shuffled and whispered. The entire village must have heard their pitiful stirrings, but no one else made a sound all night. We all seemed to be waiting for morning, hoping daylight might illuminate a path. At daybreak, Mama and Gilbert were still asleep, and Papa was gone. A wisp of smoke curled from our fire pit.

I wanted to stay in the village, to be with my family as they dealt with their confusion and anger. I wanted to ease their pain and assuage my conscience. I thought I could somehow protect the women in the hut from the villagers' misguided rage, that I could help the people of my village to realize that harming these women could never compensate their loss, that by hurting these women they would only cause themselves more pain.

But I was tired, and I was afraid of what was about to happen. I knew I could just leave and go to Kefamo. I could avoid the uncertainty for a while. I could take time to think and talk and reenergize before trying again to confront my family. Plagued by doubt and crippled by guilt, I slipped through the door and crept out of the village.

I watched the condensation drift from the roofs of the huts, except the one imprisoning the women. It sat cold and dormant, as though the flame within it had already been extinguished.

I left the village and started down the trail.

The air seemed particularly hazy that morning, as a low clouds cascaded across the mountain. As I walked, I wondered whether I was still asleep and dreaming. I toyed with the idea that none of it had happened, that the last couple of days had been a dream. Maybe Aha-no was fine, crouched before his hut, a newspaper-rolled cigarette rolled in newspaper perched between his lips, watching me stumble down the trail, grinning patiently as I made my awkward way, hoping by sheer will that he could help me to grasp what was happening around me.

But at the bluff where his hut stood, there was only the empty clearing and the restless sky above it.

We studied Pidgin in the morning, and after a drowsy lunch I went to the library in hopes of sleeping. The silence seemed oppressive, and I couldn't relax. The slightest sounds pulled me from sleep. People outside laughed; the breeze rustled across the lawns. The clock on the library wall ticked away the seconds toward eternity.

The shock of Aha-no's death had worn off, and with it went my disbelief. I accepted now that he was gone, and I acknowledged not only his loss, but also that the response of my village was real. There was no denying the dread that now occupied the village. They intended to kill these women.

I felt an obligation, to my family as much as to the women. I couldn't let them do this. As much as I wanted to protect the women from the villagers, I also thought I could protect the villagers from themselves, because I believed that by destroying these women, they would be destroying something in themselves, some intrinsic innocence I perceived them to have, perceived us all to have, until we lose it. Until we destroy it. When innocence is gone, it's gone. There's no getting it back.

In retrospect, I realize my notion of their purity was no less naïve than their exaggerated view of my stature as a Westerner and a white man. They were just as capable of tarnishing themselves as I was. As much as I feared what they would do to the women, I feared what it would do to me. My idea, or my idealization, of them should never have determined my reaction to what was happening there. But I didn't know if I was trying to protect the women, or if I only sought to make myself feel better.

The day dragged. In language lessons, we role-played going to the market or asking for directions. Later, I sat with Dieter, Mike, Brent, and Dave, and we discussed the women in the hut in speculative terms. Brent compared the situation to the concepts of game theory he had learned in economics class, the Prisoner's Dilemma and the Nash Equilibrium.

"Two people are taken prisoner, accused of the same crime," he said. "The authorities realize they couldn't both have done it, so they need to figure out who did. They separate the prisoners and give them each three options. The first is, if each accuses the other, while maintaining his own innocence, then each gets a life sentence. The second option is, if each maintains that *neither* is guilty, then each gets a lighter sentence, say twenty years. The third option is, if one accuses the other, while maintaining his own innocence, and the other continues to insist that *both* are innocent, then the one who makes the accusation goes free and the other is put to death. See how it works?"

"Not really," Mike spoke for us all.

"The point is, manipulating the consequences removes the importance of who is actually responsible. It's got nothing to do with right or wrong or who did what," Brent explained. "The dilemma is that the most equitable solution doesn't appeal to either person. If both claim that neither is guilty, then neither is killed, but both are punished equally. But if one accuses the other and the other *doesn't* accuse him, the accuser goes free and the accused is killed. The *only* option in the end is to accuse the other person. If you don't, you're exposed. So, standing by the truth has no practical function," Brent said. "It doesn't matter."

My head spun as I tried to relate this academic theory to the women in the hut, but it was all too abstract, too remote. And what did it matter? We knew that eventually the women would turn on each other. It was the only way to end the situation. The only question was, who would be the one to turn?

Truth gets distorted every day, by perception, bias, even memory. But it had never confused me so much. There were no ethics by which the women in that hut should determine their actions. The value of truth for them had been negated. Right and wrong had been usurped by circumstance.

It wasn't supposed to work that way. Morality shouldn't be subjective. It shouldn't matter what else is happening; what's right should be apparent and should show us where to go. But it didn't. There was no way out.

* * *

I didn't hurry back to the village that evening. I thumbed through books in the library and avoided the eventuality of my return. When I finally caught a PMV, the driver worried about me walking the trail in the dark, and he took us off-road to ascend the path.

We drove in silence through the hushed evening, and as daylight dispersed beyond the vague horizon, I was afforded a few moments of precious anonymity, shielded in darkness from the stares of my fellow passengers, mostly sellers returning from the market. When the PMV groaned to a halt, the bridge lay before us, bathed in the chalky illumination of the misaligned headlights. I assured him I was fine from there.

I climbed out and watched the van easing in reverse down the narrow path. Soon it disappeared around a bend, and I began to make my way across the bridge, following the milky beam of my flashlight.

In a way, it was easier to cross the bridge at night, because I couldn't see the chasm below it, or the meager timbers that held it in place. Not seeing, not knowing, made the crossing an almost fatalistic leap of faith, to which it was easier to commit because the potential outcomes were indefinite.

At the other side, a hushed voice called: "Nipi'e."

I couldn't see anything in the darkness. "Who's there?"

"It's Tim," said the voice. "Are you alright, brother?"

"I'm alright," I answered. "What are you doing here?"

"*Lukautim*," was all he said. "Watching."

It occurred to me that the families of the women might come for them. I hadn't thought about it before, but the women must have *wantoks*, people who cared for them. I imagined how the people of my village would react if two of their women were taken and locked in a hut somewhere, threatened, tormented. They would hurl themselves to the defense of their women with all their might. Were the people of my village prepared for the *wantoks* of these women to do the same? Yet here Tim stood a lonely watch, on his own. He wouldn't be able to do any more than shout a warning if attackers came.

"Are the women still there?" I asked.

"Just one," he said. "The one who followed us home from Soti's wedding."

In the distance, a lark let loose its peculiar call.

"And the other one?"

"Our people asked questions of the women today. One said the other was a witch, that she killed Aha-no. We let that woman go, and we kept the witch."

I exhaled. "She was scared, Tim," I said. "She would say anything."

"No," Tim insisted. "She told us what happened."

I shook my head. "What will happen now?"

He didn't have an answer. "You should go," he suggested. "Your Mama and Papa are worried for you. They said you should have been home earlier. They are afraid that you aren't coming back. But I am glad you're here, Nipi'e." I felt his hand pat my shoulder as I turned to walk toward the village.

Since being taken captive, the women had both denied culpability in Aha-no's death. That made it more difficult for the villagers to act. The women depended on one another, and I had hoped that if both had maintained the truth, both could be freed. But now their unity was gone, and the people of my village had all the corroboration they needed.

I climbed the gate and crossed the *singsing* ground. Splinters of light stabbed through the cracks in the walls of the neighboring huts. I opened our door to find the fire burning high, though dinnertime had passed. Mama sat at the hearth, feeding yams to Gilbert. Surprised, she stood to put her hand on my arm.

"Nipi'e!" she said. "My boy has come home."

Papa emerged into the light of the fire, looking relieved.

"Your Mama was afraid," he said. "You are home late."

I apologized for worrying them, and I sat beside the fire pit. "Tim said one of the women is gone." They only looked at me, and I pressed on. "You can't believe what she said, Papa. It doesn't mean anything."

"*Em no wari bilong yu,*" he said. "It's not your problem."

"Papa, this is wrong. You can't…"

He interrupted me and repeated, with a harshness he had never used with me before, "It's not your worry!" His voice softened. "Please, Nipi'e."

The hut fell to silence again, the only sound the cracking of the fire. I lowered my head. "I'm tired," I conceded. "I should sleep."

"Yes," Papa agreed, "it's no good if you're tired. It will be better tomorrow."

I believed him, either because he had convinced me or because he himself

126

believed it. But I sat on the floor and pulled slid off my boots, my shirt, and my shorts. As I pulled my mosquito net aside and ducked beneath it, Papa called to me.

"Nipi'e," he said. "Good night."

I nodded, and I stewed in my silent disappointment, in him and in myself. What else could I say?

How could I teach what I believed was right and wrong, to Papa or anyone else? What did I really have to teach them? Was I any different from any of those who had trespassed on this place before me to impose on these people a way of life that was anathema to them, to everything they had ever known? Pulled them in every direction, convinced them to let go of all they had been taught to believe and value?

Could I play upon the same neuroses and naiveté that had facilitated the missionaries and bred the cargo cults?

Could I convince them their only deliverance was to be like me?

How could I presume to teach anything about spiritual or philosophical principle? How could I dictate morality? What did I know about it? Where would I have learned it? Was it hiding somewhere in the hypocrisy and judgment of the church where we reluctantly spent those frigid Sunday mornings in Green Bay? Was it in the family I had neglected, or the education I had squandered? Could I turn aside all the doubts, misgivings and second thoughts I had about why I came to this place, and allow these circumstances to determine my path and the nature of my relationship with the people here?

The fire had begun to wane, and Papa's face looked faded from across the hut. I turned and lowered my head, hoping I would sleep, but knowing I would not.

December 21, 1994 – Solutions

That night passed in uneasy silence, with little to mark the passage of time aside from an occasional rustling from the nearby hut. Now and again throughout the night I found myself awake, my eyes open, staring at the mesh of my mosquito net or the frayed stitching of my sleeping bag, vaguely aware. But those were isolated moments. I couldn't tell what happened between them, or if I had been awake or asleep. I had no answers. I only knew that, with all of us as tired as we were, the village remained anxious.

In the cold light of early dawn, a twitching shadow caught the corner of my eye, and I turned to watch a cockroach crawling along the floor, its long antennae weaving a deliberate and graceful pattern through the air before it. It negotiated the hills and valleys of the thatched bamboo, and I waited without moving. As it approached me, unaware, I slowly pulled aside the edge of my mosquito net, and when it came near enough, I slammed my fist on top of it, and then stared at the lifeless form.

Empty moments passed as I regarded the dead bug, until a black ant came along the same trail the roach had followed. When the ant came upon the cockroach, it immediately began surveying the body, crawling around its edges, up and over it again and again, its movements erratic, jerky. Then it scurried away.

More time passed until the ant returned, accompanied now by dozens of others, and they swarmed over the carcass, first inspecting the job at hand and then tearing with their pincers at fragments of head, wings, legs and thorax, cutting the parts loose, holding them aloft and turning to make their way back to wherever they had come from.

The ants worked in two lines, single file. One carted away segments of the cockroach while the other returned for another trip. I lay there in my sleeping bag and watched, engrossed, as the ants systematically and dispassionately tore apart the remnants of what had previously been a living thing but now, within a few moments, had been fundamentally deconstructed into its disparate parts.

The grotesque dance played out before me as if it were meant for me to see, as if these insects were not just following the rote instinct of a hundred million years of evolution but were instead trying to tell me something. Like Francis' goat, turned inside out, exposing its secret– if only I could see it for what it was. As if showing me the separate components of the cockroach exposed nature's hidden internal contradictions, subverted their significance, defrayed their unity, and shattered their order. This dismantling, this dissection – was it for my edification? A part of my catechism?

When the ants had finished, not so much as a smudge remained. A few moments were all it took to obliterate any evidence the cockroach had ever existed. All that remained was an impression, an image, a dream imprinted on my memory, where it will remain for the rest of my life.

What should become of the things we remember?

The cicadas had begun to drone, and I slowly emerged from my sleeping bag. I stood and dressed, stepped across the floor and over the smoldering fire pit, lifted the latch on the door and ducked outside. It hadn't rained the night before, and though it was still early, the air had grown oppressive. It was going to be a hot day.

I was dusty and sweaty when I arrived in Kefamo. Barry met me as I passed his office. "Any updates?" he asked.

"They let one go," I responded, shaking my head. "She said the other one was a witch. Said she killed Aha-no."

Barry didn't look surprised.

"I suppose this is it," I mumbled.

He pointed toward the kitchen. "Get something to eat," he said, calmly. "I'll catch up with you in a little while." He headed to the classroom.

The dining room sat almost empty. A couple of the other volunteers were

129

scattered along the tables, looking tired and muddy. I walked through to the library, where I found Mike, Dieter, Brent, and Dave. We had settled into a habit of gathering there most mornings to play cards before the day's sessions.

I sat at the table, and the others made a space for me. Mike flipped a card, then asked, "What's happening in your village?"

I told them about the previous night, and they nodded. "So I guess they're gonna do it," I finally said. I arranged my cards, seeking comfort in the simplicity of order. "I feel like I shouldn't let this happen. But I don't know what I can do to stop it." I tossed a card.

"Everyone knows what's going on up there," Dave said, "and nobody's doing anything about it. No one in your village is gonna get in any trouble."

"Even if they did," I said, "she'd still be dead."

"So, the question is," Dieter said, "how do you face them?"

I held my card poised and shook my head. "They don't want me to be around if they do this, and they don't want to talk to me about it. They just want to go on like we did before. And I guess, so do I."

Dave nodded and played his card. Mike dropped his and took the trick. "Can you?" he asked, throwing his next card. They all looked at me.

"I don't know," I said. "They are gonna do this." I thumped my card on the table, harder than was necessary. "And nobody cares. So how do I go back there?"

Nobody had an answer.

I was anxious to return to my village, but I dreaded it at the same time. Throughout the day I went to our training sessions, thinking it might take my mind off things, but instead I found myself sitting and staring at my hands. Waiting.

I avoided conversation about what would happen and how I might respond. I couldn't put words to the jumble of emotions roiling through me, and it frustrated me to try. A few people asked about it, thinking it might help me to talk it through, but I turned away their questions. Nobody pushed.

I had tried that morning to find some relief in talking to my friends, but my return to normality had been disorienting. Now, I was irritated by people laughing or speaking in animated tones about village life, or about the intricacies of communication in the villages. Suddenly, it all struck me as pathetically naïve. What did we think we were doing here? What difference did we think we were making?

The others picked up on my reluctance and kept their distance as I sat alone and waited for the day to drift away so I could return to my village. I stewed in indecision and remorse for something that hadn't yet happened.

That afternoon, I sat in Barry's office, glancing at the same newspaper folded at the edge of his desk, reporting the football scores from two months ago. It seemed like time had stopped.

"We've talked with the office in Moresby," Barry told me, "about what's going on up in your village. They called out to Peace Corps headquarters in Washington."

At this, I looked up. It stunned me to know people 10,000 miles away were discussing the tiny cluster of mountain huts that had been my home these past weeks.

He drew a breath and continued. "They want to pull you out. Tonight. Told me to send Sonny up to get your stuff."

I didn't know what to say. "Where would I go?"

"You'd finish out training here at Kefamo," he responded.

That was it. An answer, of sorts. I could leave and not look back. Like my daydreams of flying, being somewhere else. No responsibility, no obligation. I could just walk away. In fact, I was being told to walk away. No stigma, no stink of failure. It would be over. Not for her, or for anyone else up there. But it would be over for me.

"It's up to you," Barry continued. "What do you want to do?"

For a moment, I allowed myself to consider spending the remaining weeks of my training amid the relative comforts of Kefamo: hot showers instead of a cold and muddy stream; indoor plumbing and a porcelain commode instead of a hole in the ground; a soft bed instead of a moldy sleeping bag; eggs and bacon for breakfast instead of tea and sweet potatoes; electricity, plumbing, privacy, solitude.

I wouldn't even have to face my family. Sonny would go to the village– his

131

village– to collect my things and explain that I wouldn't be returning. I could almost see him tiptoeing around the inside of the hut, trying not to wake Gilbert. Taking down the mosquito net Papa had so carefully hung. Rolling up my sleeping bag, collecting my things, while my family watched, awaiting an explanation that wouldn't come.

But even as I envisioned leaving, I knew I wouldn't. I couldn't. I had followed that path before, and I knew where it led. I wanted this to be different. I wanted to face whatever happened in my village. I wanted to face my host family, no matter what they did. I would return to Mari-eka that night, and the next night, too, until my time there was finished.

I looked at Barry and shook my head. "I don't want to leave," I told him. "I want to stay up there."

He nodded. "Listen," he said, "the Peace Corps not going to get involved in what's happening in your village. Do you understand that?" He watched me intently. "They won't stop what's going to happen up there. Nobody will."

I nodded. "If they do this," I said, "I mean, if the people in my village kill that woman, what will happen to them?"

"What do you mean?" he asked.

"You said there were laws against sorcery, to keep people from taking matters into their own hands. Well, that's what's happening in my village, isn't it? They're taking matters into their own hands. So," I asked again, "what will happen to them?"

He slowly shook his head. "The authorities in Goroka might investigate, but they won't push it. Cops here are tribesmen first. They're more faithful to tradition and custom than to the laws of the outside world."

"What about the woman's village?" I asked. "Her family? Won't anyone come looking for her? Won't they do something about this?"

Barry's expression offered little hope. "I doubt it."

I shook my head. "Seriously?"

"The fact is," he said, "she's a woman in her late forties. No husband, no children. Soon enough, she would become a drain on the resources of her village, if she isn't already an economic liability. Someone who no longer pulls her weight." He shrugged his shoulders. "She'd be a burden."

"So, her own people will let this happen?" I asked.

"They believe in *sanguma*, too, ah?" he said. "They may believe she really is a witch. But look, the point is this: are you sure you want to want to go back up there?"

I nodded. He seemed to be waiting for more, but I shrugged. "I have to," was all I could muster. It wasn't much of an explanation, but it was enough. Barry seemed to understand.

That evening, I climbed the path to Mari-eka as a steady breeze fanned away the lingering humidity, trailing a high cover of thick cloud that diminished the late afternoon sun. With the haze gone, the view of the distant peaks was stunning, but I hardly noticed. The beauty of nature drifted past and faded behind me. Even the bridge and the chasm beneath it left me unfazed.

The *singsing* ground sat empty and still. Thickening clouds of approaching rain made the evening light dim, and from across the village, I could make out no more than the shapes of the huts, obscured by scarce light and smoke from cooking fires. Coming closer, I strained to see the hut where the women had been held. The door sat open, framing a black, empty interior.

The door to our hut swung open to reveal Papa standing in the frame. His voice was calm, but strained. "Nipi'e," he said. "It's time to eat."

I gestured at the empty hut. "Where is she?"

He ignored my question. "Tonight, we say goodbye to Aha-no," he said. "The ceremony will start soon."

Mama sat nursing Gilbert. "My boy is home," she said, smiling as I sat on a stone at the hearth's edge and accepted a yam, charred by the fire.

"What happened?" I asked.

Mama shifted Gilbert in her lap. Papa wouldn't answer. "Eat quickly," he instructed me. "We will go soon."

I crouched before the fire and ate the steaming yam. I knew that if Papa wouldn't tell me happened, someone else would. I was certain everyone knew.

As I ate, Papa paced around the perimeter of the fire. He was nervous, and I felt a strange mix of satisfaction and shame at the thought that I might be partly the cause of his unease. In silence, I ate a few more bites, and then we left, following the same route we had followed the night Aha-no died, passing through the *singing* ground, climbing the gate and crossing the trail toward the bluff.

The sky had darkened, and rain had begun to fall. A bonfire raged in the pit before Aha-no's hut.

"The women put mud on their faces, to show sadness," Papa explained amid the unabashed crying of the mourners. "We will burn Aha-no's body, along with his clothes and all of his things. We will dig up his garden and remove everything growing there."

It was a way of saying goodbye. A release of their sorrow and his spirit, a symbolic letting go, a statement that it was time to move on. I looked at the remnants of the old man's garden. A fence that had kept pigs at bay had been dismantled, and the soil of the little plot was raw and upturned, the disarray illuminated by the light of the fire.

A few dozen people were there; both men and women, dark arms pulled tight against drawn, pitiful chests. Their bodies shook and spasmed as they cried. The mud on the women's faces fell in tiny clumps, flicked loose by drops of rain.

Mama joined the circle at the fire. She had wiped mud across her face, too, thick and heavy on her swollen cheeks. She swayed with the others and wailed, and Gilbert, confused and frightened, bawled softly. She tucked his head against her shoulder and rocked him as she cried.

I have always viewed crying as a personal expression, carried out in solitude, even hidden in shame. But in this place, crying was a collective experience, a group outpouring, conducted in unison by an entire village. Everyone cried, some holding one another, others pacing the flat surface before Aha-no's hut. They cried unreservedly, without shame, shoulders shaking, hands flung repeatedly at their sides.

I was awed by the desperate anguish of their sorrow. The sound they made was almost deafening, a group catharsis; full, deep, rhythmic, even energetic. Watching the ritual of their grief, I felt I should be somewhere– anywhere– else. I backed away from the circle and crouched at the edge of the clearing, beneath a ficus tree, as if it might hide me.

I didn't see any structure to the ceremony: no one presided, and very little happened. The men turned to the sky, eyes closed, and bellowed with ferocity and sorrow. The women shuffled their feet and flung their arms. Their hands flayed in a crazy rhythm, as if they were trying to physically shake the sorrow from their bodies like grains of earth.

I recognized most of the people in the crowd, as the rain soaked their faces, making their skin shine by the light of the fire. Francis was there, and when he noticed me, he gave a small nod. Tim came and shook my hand.

Then, I felt a sudden, heavy hand grasp my shoulder, and I turned to find Elvis grinning at me, his face too close to mine. "Nipi'e," he said, "It is good you are here."

I only nodded and turned back the fire and the mourners. He fell into a seated position beside me, and from the corner of my eye, I saw him staring at me.

"We killed her," he told me in a plain voice, and I almost didn't believe him, because I didn't want to, or because he made it sound so easy. The wailing mourners who shook and turned before me became a backdrop to his hoarse voice. "Today we punished her for what she did."

He was proud of it, and I knew he would tell me everything. People don't lie well when they're drunk.

"How?"

"You want to know?" he asked, pleased with my interest. He spoke slowly and evenly in Pidgin, to make sure I understood. "We took her to the edge of the village and hung her by her neck." A twitching grin crept across his mouth. "We made a fire underneath her, and we burned her."

The wailing of the mourners engulfed us.

"We cut at her with bush-knives," he said. I waited for more. "Now it is finished."

Stunned by the brutality he described, I wondered if the act had anything at all to do with the woman herself, whom the people of my village barely knew. Revenge wasn't the right word for what they did, and neither was compensation. It wasn't the woman they attacked, it was something deeper, more profound– an abstraction, a bogey man, an embodiment of anger, hate and despair. They made her a symbol, an effigy. That is how they were able to dehumanize and annihilate her. She became a representation and a repository of all their fears.

135

Suddenly, Papa's voice broke through the sounds of the mourners' cries. "Elvis!" he shouted.

Both of us snapped our heads toward the sound of Papa's voice, and Elvis smiled. "My brother," he said. He tried to get up, but staggered and grabbed my shoulder to keep his balance. I twisted from his hand, and he fell face-first to the wet earth.

Papa lunged at him and lifted him by the collar of a dead anthropologist's colorful winter coat. I stood to move aside and saw that Elvis' face, like those of the women around the fire, was covered in mud, and when he smiled, it dripped into his mouth and smeared across his jagged teeth.

Papa could barely contain his fury. "Go!" he shouted, and he maneuvered Elvis to the edge of the plateau and shoved him. Elvis fell down the slope, tumbling through the wet *kunai* grass. At the bottom, he staggered into the darkness, cursing.

Papa turned back to me, and we stared at each other through the dim night. He looked exhausted, feeble, as if there were nothing left in him. Finally, without speaking, he turned from me and rejoined the others at the fire.

They wailed and chanted into the uncaring night, and I watched from my perch, oblivious to the rain and the mud, my mind replaying what Elvis had told me. My friends, my adoptive family, who danced and cried as blurred images before me, had murdered a woman.

I sat on the ground and lowered my head, breathing deeply, hoping to exhale the regret and the remorse, exorcise it all. Tears ran slowly down my cheeks, absorbed with the rain into my beard. I sat alone beneath the tree, and I cried. I cried for the death of a tired old man, and a frightened, helpless woman. I cried, too, for those who killed her, and I cried for myself, a very, very long way from home.

Exhaustion washed over me along with the rain, and I closed my eyes as the drops streamed down my face. Tension seeped from me, and I wept in silence, and in relief, because now it was over. At some point, I fell asleep against the tree.

Later, Papa woke me. The rain had turned to a fine mist, and most of the mourners were gone. Those who remained were silent. They stood around the fire, the smoke twirling through the haze into the dark sky.

"He is gone," Papa said. The flames popped and crackled, the embers glowing and beginning to die.

"I'm sorry, Papa," I mumbled.

"It is late," he turned to face me. "Your Mama is home already."

No words passed between us as we walked home; there were none to say. Our footsteps slogged through the mud, the sounds trapped in the fog and the still air.

Inside, I crawled beneath my mosquito net and lay my head on the bamboo floor. Papa left the lamp burning, and I stared at the ceiling. Tired as I felt, I couldn't fall asleep. Some ember, deep inside me, refused to go out.

I tried to remember what the woman had looked like the day we met, or the day she waved to me from the market, or the times I had seen her around the village, but nothing came to me. I could only think of the outrage and indignation she must have felt.

But maybe I was wrong. Maybe she didn't feel anything. I wondered if there was some point where the brain disassociates itself from pain and fear, and convinces itself not to register them. At the brink of its demise, is it possible for intellect to overcome instinct and comprehend, on a primal level, that there is no way to stop its suffering, that for the remainder of its existence, there will be nothing else? Can we, in some way, take pain for granted, accept the inevitability and the immediacy of our end, and disconnect ourselves from our own cries for help?

People desperately want to believe that everything falls into the plans of nature, that there is a logic and a structure and thus some meaning or design behind it. But maybe the simple whim of fate and fortune means that there are only a select few beings who can experience contentment, while the rest of the animal kingdom passes its time on earth in a succession of anxiety and fear. Maybe a whale, a mammal that by some ridiculous quirk of circumstance has been banished to a life in the water, knows nothing but the struggle to find its next breath. Just because it knows nothing else, that doesn't mean it likes what it knows. How does it accept what it is?

Was it somehow possible the woman was destined for this end? Was this her appointment in Sammara, a fate to which her entire life had led? Could she have known this? Could she have watched and simply accepted, as they went about the work of her murder? What would have occupied her final thoughts? Where could her mind have found refuge in those last moments? Did her life flash before her, as they say it does, a flow of distinct images, or the single culmination of all her days up to that one, everything compressed to that instant, all she had ever seen, heard, felt? What were the things she remembered? Did she find comfort in them?

I wondered where my own mind would turn, what I would remember. I tried to convince myself that, if faced with what she faced, I would seek in my waning moments for goodness, love, and splendor and for warmth, softness, contentment. The purity of youth, when a child still believes the world is a safe place where nothing can go wrong. Could I draw upon the moments of profound comfort I'd had the privilege to know in my life? Would I remember dangling my feet alongside my friends from a railroad bridge above the Susquehanna River? Listening to my mother read to me as I lay tucked beneath the covers of my bed, as the winds of a Wisconsin winter howled outside my window? Sitting with my father, sharing a glass of orange juice as we watched the sun rise over the Grand Canyon? Staying up all night with my college roommates, surrounded by empty beer bottles and pizza boxes, gazing at a world that seemingly lay at our feet? The instances of my life when I was implicitly happy.

Years ago.

Thousands of miles away.

An eternity.

A lifetime.

Someone else's lifetime. I wondered if, dying, she dreamed of beauty.

December 22, 1994 – Requiem

Eventually, I stumbled into a thick, dreamless sleep. Regret and culpability nagged at me from a distance, but for a few hours, fatigue overcame emotion. In the calm and silent wake of her murder, I slept.

The next morning, I sat before the cooking fire, sucking the pulpy seeds from a passion fruit. Papa sat opposite me, nursing a cup of tea. We didn't speak.

It had been a while since I had sat in such intimacy with my host family. Now, it felt unfamiliar. We had become strangers again.

"Nipi'e," Mama called in a subdued voice, "our rice is finished."

I nodded. "I'll go to town this afternoon and get more."

"You are a good boy," she told me. "Hurry home. You need your rest. Tomorrow you and your Papa will *wokabout*."

I glanced at Papa, and he nodded. "We start early," he said, his hands wrapped around a tin mug. "It's a little bit of a long way, but you are fit. I know you can make it."

We sat in silence, listening to the cracks of the cooking fire and watching the embers shift. Then I glanced at my watch. "It's time for me to go," I said.

I walked slowly across the *singing* ground, noticing the tranquility brought by the passing of an evening of peace. The village still slept, and the huts sat in hushed serenity. Wilbur stepped aside for me that morning without so much as a grunt.

I descended the trail in a fog, confused by the emptiness of my sentiments. I couldn't bring myself to feel anything but relief. What they'd done was worse than I had even imagined, and I felt complicit, because I hadn't stopped them.

But how could I? I was in a different world.

That wasn't enough to excuse my inaction, though. I wasn't prepared to write this off as a mere cultural difference. I thought that what I had developed with my host family went beyond differences in the way we looked, the way we spoke, the way we dressed. I couldn't just tell myself that I had to accept what they had done because this was their culture and I would never understand it– that would be an admission that our relationship never overcome that obstacle in the first place.

I didn't want to confront the fact that the people of my village had done something terrible, because I thought it would be a *de facto* implication that they themselves were terrible people. And I knew they weren't. So it didn't add up; it didn't make sense, and I couldn't make sense of it. So, I tried to push it out of my mind, like a child pushing away his homework because he cannot get the equations and algorithms to come together.

I wasn't yet prepared to face the notion that we all have a little of this in us. I couldn't allow myself to believe there is innate corruption in us all. Maybe that, more than the petty hypocrisy of the sad little church my family used to attend, was why I rebelled so strenuously against my Catholic upbringing. I couldn't accept the notion that we are born with primal immorality, that we enter this world from the moment of our conception tainted by sin.

I could never accept this as a stricture of faith. I don't believe that we must all confess to some inherent wickedness, and exorcise it in the suffering of someone else, in order to actualize our relationship with the divine and achieve salvation. This can't be how we bring ourselves closer to a god.

Yet the ideology must have imprinted itself on my psyche more deeply than I had realized, because it came to fundamentally inform the way I viewed what happened in my village.

In the years since, I have come to recognize that, in my memory and in my imagination, I made the woman a martyr, as if her ritual sacrifice was an attempt to atone for collective guilt. Maybe that was why I couldn't – and cannot – alleviate my sense of culpability in what happened to her.

I walked along the trail, as the berrypeckers and longbills whistled and trilled to one another. Rivulets of rusty water meandered back and forth, tumbling to the streams and rivers that carved the steep Highland valleys. The air had begun to warm, turning the mist into a blanket of humidity, heavy with the scents of sun-warmed grass, manure, and wood smoke. A light breeze accompanied me as I walked, insisting that the world remained a beautiful place.

After classes at Kefamo, I made my way to a trade store in town to get some rice, as Mama had asked. I picked up a few more cans of mackerel and a jar of tea, and I refilled our jug of kerosene. Jostled by the crowds, I hoisted my purchases over my shoulder to return to the street and the curious stares of passersby. I made my way to the PMV stop and waited there.

I was struck by the earthy concoction of body odor, cement dust, acrid smoke from trash-burning fires and the tart scent of *buai* and *kambang*. The breeze should have dissipated the odors; but it only pressed them more insistently in my face. I felt caustic and standoffish, wanting to retreat into my own world and escape the masses and redolence of this one.

Eventually, a Toyota Coaster approached and groaned to a halt. The door swung open, and I squinted through the dust to ask the driver if he was going toward Daulo Pass. He nodded without looking at me, and I welcomed his disinterest as I climbed aboard. I adjusted my purchases, which jutted so high I could barely see around them. As I set the things aside, I suddenly realized all the other passengers on the bus were nuns.

"Jesus," I muttered, and one of them absently crossed herself.

The habit of their order was a pale gray skirt trimmed with white, a plain white shirt and a gray vest. They wore a wimple around their shoulders and a cornette with a curved brim that made them look like some species of ungainly, exotic fowl. They were Highland *meris*, who had exchanged one form of *bilas* for another. They had round, dark faces adorned with tribal tattoos that disappeared behind their head coverings. A few glanced at me, but none for long. They seemed almost surreal, but by now I was developing a certain familiarity with alternative realities.

I settled beside the driver and stared through the window, its cracked pane rattling in its frame as the engine wheezed and the bus picked up speed. The suspension was *bagarap*, and we bounced and jarred along the pocked dirt road that accessed the Highlands Highway.

As we made our way, a voice behind me began speaking smoothly and steadily, the tone almost conversational, but also undeniably lyrical. I couldn't make out her words over the growling of the bus, and she spoke in a *tok ples* different even from the one spoken in my village. Still, I felt something inherently soothing in her cadence and tone, and I allowed the sound to caress the recesses of my consciousness.

Then, one of the others added her voice to the first, complementing rather than interrupting, the rhythms and tones overlapping and blending. It was only then I realized they weren't talking. They were singing.

When they finished the first phrase, they left a gap filled by the labored stutter of the diesel engine straining for a higher gear. Then the women began again, and this time, the others joined them. Their song was neither joyful nor sad. Instead, it seemed to describe an ambiguous emotion unlike anything I could have recognized before coming to this place: benign, unassuming and gentle, but hinting at some distant darkness– not confronting it, just acknowledging it. As the voices came together as one, their tone perfectly complemented the notes of the song, as if they were made by nature to be united, and what resulted was an exquisite sense of gentle melancholy, a perfect composite of love, loss, living, breathing, flying and falling; a dizzying amalgam of all that make up what it is to be, and my heart stirred like a child's and the flesh on my arms rose, because I had never in my life heard anything so beautiful.

I turned to find each of the nuns staring out of a window, or at her hands clasped in her lap, as the bus lurched along the road on its buggered suspension, causing the covered heads to bob and loll like human metronomes. All the while, their part in the song seemed almost incidental, as if they just happened to be singing, but were really more concerned with the obsidian shadows of the rainforest passing their mud-smeared windows, or with the stitching of the seatback in front of them.

Despite the distracted way they sang, there was a poignancy and resplendence to the blending of their voices. It was instinctual, reflexive, and they seemed no more aware of it than they were of their own breathing. They sang with the same lack of self-consciousness as Francis' children, but for these women, this was not a performance. I doubt it occurred to them someone might be listening, and had they known I was, they might have stopped. So, I turned again to face the road before us, because the last thing in the world I wanted was for them to stop.

I suppose in some way I took their song as a eulogy for Aha-no. He might even have appreciated the irony of it, after all his resistance to the machinery of Christianity. But the song could just as easily have been for the accused woman, victimized by the misguided rage of my village. Or maybe they didn't sing as nuns at all, but simply as Highland women, the only other people who could empathize with her fate.

The trace of melancholy in their song perfectly fit my own nagging sense of loss and sadness. I'd been consumed by the guilt of what happened, and I felt resentful of the other volunteers and townspeople who laughed and carried on as if they didn't have a care in the world. I found in the palliative refrain of the nuns' song that someone did care, and they, like me, recognized this darkness. They feared it, too, and together they sought some way through it. In that moment, we weren't alone.

I know there is a place in the realm of comprehension where the value of words is not enough. Some things have no designation in human diction, regardless of the intricacy of the language or the eloquence of the speaker. Likewise, I have no faith in religion or superstition – music is the closest thing to magic I believe in. In those instances where there are no words, there is music.

And on that day, in a battered bus, lugging a sack of rice, a few cans of fish and a bottle of kerosene, wondering where the next few days and weeks would lead, the efficacy of words abandoned me, replaced by the poignant lyricism and pure magic of a dozen nuns, whose careless singing more accurately approximated my own emotion than any words ever could.

Soon, the bus slowed to a halt before the trail to Mari-eka. The women stopped singing, and I reluctantly gathered my belongings and climbed down to the muddied trailhead. I paid the driver and searched the noncommittal expression of his face, but again found nothing. He swung the door closed, jammed the bus into gear and pulled away.

The windows of the Coaster paraded before me, framing the faces of the nuns one by one as the bus rolled past. I hoped that by some shared look I could find someone who recognized what I had witnessed, what we had shared, but the nuns just held their random, blank stares. The van disappeared over a crest in the road, and I turned and began to walk toward my village.

December 23, 1994 – Time

Papa woke me at first light. I crawled from my sleeping bag into the chill of the morning, crept to the edge of the fire pit and laced my boots as he retrieved a few tools from pegs along the wall. He handed me a shovel, and the two of us slipped through the door into a blanket of haze that embraced the entire side of the mountain. Just a few feet before me, Papa was a blurred outline, a barefoot apparition with a shovel hoisted over its shoulder, striding through the fog.

The veil of cloud provided a buffer between us, and neither of us spoke. If the air had been clear, we might have felt compelled to say something to overcome the silence, but instead, there was a pathos in the mist that practically forbade us to speak, and in truth, I was grateful for it. Neither of us knew what to say.

We climbed the village gate and began walking further up the mountain. We passed among the mammoth ferns and drapes of moss, the earleaf acacias and evergreen podocarpus, with gnarled trunks and twisted branches, which stood with greater distinction against the gray tapestry of the billowing fog. Jumbled masses of vines and creepers impudently enveloped all they reached. Condensation gathered on each branch, every leaf, encasing them in crystalline beads that rolled across the leaves' surface to cling to the edge for an instant before dropping to the clay soil.

The burden of the pervasive moisture forced the branches to sag toward the ground in feeble supplication, as if bowing before a disinterested master. They drooped to the brink of collapse, tilting toward the forest floor at untenable angles, yet they didn't fall. Their porous, pliable trunks absorbed moisture like sponges, and no matter how prone they were, they clung to the soil and fought for every scrap of air, every sliver of light, a mute struggle for survival in an environment seemingly bent on their destruction.

Our footsteps sent animals scurrying through the underbrush, and the birds of the rainforest gave constant warnings, their shrill calls a bizarre, disembodied mix of echoing whistles, shrieks and clicks. One sounded like the taunting, hysterical laughter of a crazed woman, like the women who danced and embraced my legs on the day I arrived in the village, and several times I thought to point out the sound and ask Papa to identify the bird that made it, but I couldn't overcome the weight of the silence between us.

Eventually, the fog could no longer compete with the rising sun, and the shroud began to dissipate. By then, we'd settled into a steady pace, maintaining our silence. Papa occasionally called out to the owner of the land we were crossing or mumbled a few words to me about a plant or animal we saw along the way. Aside from that, we didn't say anything.

We climbed hills and ridges, descended slopes blanketed in *kunai*, and crossed creeks and streams. Morning wore on and the temperature rose, sweat ran down my back, and I felt alternately tired and energized. But I wouldn't ask Papa to slow the pace. I still hated the idea of showing myself to be less than his estimation of me. Less, I suppose, than what I believed he wanted me to be.

His approval still mattered to me. I still strove to show him I was worthy of all his village had given me. Instead of emphasizing the gap between us, I only wanted to close it, to somehow make things right between us.

Eventually, we arrived at a clearing at the edge of a wide field of *kunai*, no more than an acre in the heart of a valley between two ridges. At its far edge, the clearing abutted a vertical ridge. At the center, the surface of the land was dotted by a cluster of evenly spaced *kau kau* mounds. The stalks sprouted from the mounds and crept along the ground, their yellow-green leaves splayed against rich soil.

I asked Papa whose garden it was.

"It's ours," he told me. "So many people have come to say goodbye to Aha-no, and we have been feeding them all; we need what is here."

We set our *bilums* at the edge of the clearing and Papa jammed his shovel into a mound, tamping the blade into the earth with his bare foot. After he had loosened the soil, I found the sweet potato with the tip of my machete, then pulled the vine to uproot the *kau kau* while Papa moved to the next mound.

We worked into the afternoon beneath a blazing sun and slowly gathering clouds. Birdcalls and the buzzing of insects taunted us, and our hands and knees became blackened by dirt. The encroaching mountain walls deflected the breeze, and sweat dripped from my forehead into the earthen mounds. My back ached, the sun burned my neck, and flies buzzed around my eyes and ears, unfazed by my attempts to wave them away.

I felt oddly gratified by the work, as if we were paying some sort of a penance – another lingering effect of my lapsed Catholicism. I felt, or hoped, that the ache in my back, the blisters on my hands and the sweat on my face could somehow purify me. The honesty of the soreness in my arms and the throb in my head felt good.

After a while, I took a break to crouch and pick at the blisters on my hands, and I looked at Papa. I remember watching him, stooped over a mound, working his bare hand into the soil with the precision of a heart surgeon deliberately exploring his patient's chest cavity. I couldn't decide if he was the enigma I took him to be, or if I merely recognized in him the bewildering duality of human nature, the relativity of nebulous morality, in a way I never had before.

Papa was a subsistence farmer whose garden fed his family and his community. He was a leader, a symbol of authority, wisdom, and humility. The youth of his village looked to him as an example of what it means to be a man– a model of courage and reliability, ardently faithful to his principles. He could be counted on to stand up for what he believed and to defend his family and his people.

These weren't archaic traits whose resonance had died out; his was a family and a society that *needed* defending, from all of the attacks and pressure that came from within and without. They needed a beacon, a symbol, someone in whom they could find strength and reassurance. Papa was such a man, just as Aha-no had been before him.

He was all those things. And he was a murderer.

I never knew if he fixed the rope around her neck, lit the fire beneath her feet, or swung the blade that killed her. I never asked, and I never would, because it didn't matter. He was a part of what happened to her. This man, capable of incredible strength and generosity, of wisdom and steadfastness, was also capable of true savagery.

I hated to think the word "savage" and all that it suggested. A "savage" was a fictional notion, conceived and perpetrated by colonials and missionaries, a simplified way of explaining why these people needed to be conquered and ruled, why they had not found the Lord, or been found by the Lord. I believed I knew better than to think that way. I wouldn't resort to such a simple justification for my presence among them, a convenient mask of my true motivation of service to self.

But maybe Barry was right. Maybe we weren't so different from the missionaries, mercenaries, and misfits or from the fools, freaks and failures. Maybe we have a little of all of them in each of us.

I kept coming back to my own culpability, and to the notion of collective guilt. I remembered, when I was twelve or thirteen, our church held a Good Friday service to begin the Catholic holy week. The Mass took place at night, lit only by candles, making the room almost unbearably warm and creating an air of mysticism and dread. The priest led a somber procession of parishioners, who carried a full-size wooden cross into the church and marched it reverently down the central aisle, to be placed at the altar. Then, everyone in the assembly formed a line, and each person approached, knelt, took a hammer, and pounded a nail into the cross, taking turns before the entire parish to repeat the ancient transgression.

I was just a kid, and I did as I was told, as the wavering orange glow of the candles lapped at the sloped rafters of the church ceiling. I, too, beat a nail into the rough wood, and as the sound of the hammer slamming against the nail echoed through the silent room, I was forced to envision the agony each strike would have caused. I looked at the priest, in his robes and his piety at his perch on the altar above me, and I tried to conceal my contempt as I wondered, *why are you doing this?*

But I knew the answer. The symbolism was hard to miss, even for a child who wanted with all his heart to be anywhere else. *This happened because of you,* it said, *and you are all guilty.* I remember feeling a little nauseous as I fumbled through the ambient heat of the candles to find my way back to my seat, hoping this marked the end of the Mass so we could go home.

But even afterward, laying in the safety of my bed that night, the feeling remained with me. This insane notion that this man suffered so profoundly because of me, and that I bore the burden of responsibility as much as the people who nailed him up there that day, 2,000 years ago.

I wondered how that experience would have translated to the Papua New Guinean converts to western religion. Christianity was still relatively new to the Highlands. How did the notion of original sin and collective guilt fit with animist gods, fertility ceremonies and initiation rites? How did they conflate Christian dogma with their own traditional rituals?

Christ died in a ritual, and so did the woman in my village. Jesus' followers refer to his torment and crucifixion as "the Passion," from the Latin *passionem*, meaning to suffer or endure. That passion, like the crucifix they worship, is an abiding emblem of the Christian faith in the same way the Papua New Guinean system of beliefs is represented by its own traditional customs, its own *pasin*. Passion and *pasin*; the terms seemed so close, I wondered if their commonality was mere coincidence, or something more universal.

The window had opened for an instant, and then closed again. I could almost see Barry's Cheshire cat grin.

I wondered if, as the woman's murderers went about her desecration, they felt any sense of fear and loathing, analogous to what we felt that night in our church. Rather than seeing themselves as the embodiment of sin and guilt, they projected it onto someone else, transubstantiated it into human form, then destroyed its physical incarnation in an attempt to exorcise it. But what did it give them in the end? Where did it deliver them? Did they find salvation in her sacrifice?

Finally, Papa and I had filled several *bilums* with as much *kau kau* as we could carry. It would be a long trek back to the village.

Papa built a fire at the edge of the garden and withdrew a can of corned beef and a package of hard crackers. We heated the meat over the fire, then spread it on the crackers. He took a long drink from a canister of water, then handed it to me. The water was thick and metallic. The crackers were tough, almost impossible to chew, and the corned beef was salty, strung with veins and shards of bone.

Papa cleared his throat and spoke though a mouthful of food as he gazed at the valley walls. "Aha-no helped to clear this land when he was a boy. His family had a hut nearby, but it's gone now." He looked around him, taking it in. "He liked to come back here, even when he was old, and the trip was hard. I don't know what was here for him."

"Youth," I said. Without realizing it, I had spoken the word in English, and Papa stared at me. I couldn't think of the word in Pidgin, so I rephrased. "It's the same here as it was when he was a boy. Other things changed when the outsiders came, and Aha-no changed, too. *Em kamap lapun,*" I said. *He got old.* "But when he came here it was the same as before. Maybe that made him feel good."

Papa looked about him and nodded his head. "Maybe you're right," he told me. Then he nudged the shovel against my leg and smiled. "My boy is wise."

The clouds that had been gathering since we arrived were now coming together more fully. A peal of thunder rolled through the maze of ravines that latticed the mountains. Beneath the increasing shadows, the disrupted earth in the clearing became sad, lonely. The wind carrying the coming rains cooled the air, and a familiar stillness came to this place, the moment of trepidation. Papa watched the sky with me, and together we waited.

When the rain arrived, it came with the abruptness I had become accustomed to, not as a gentle shower or an increasing drizzle but instead as a sudden downpour. Huge drops smacked against our upturned faces. We laid the sweet potatoes out to rinse in the rain, then we withdrew from the garden and sat with our backs against the cliff at the edge of the clearing, which kept us relatively dry. The rainfall was too loud to allow conversation, so I took out a pack of cards and we played a few hands of war.

Playing cards with Papa was not like playing cards with the guys at Kefamo. For us, the games were a distraction. They killed time and created a framework for conversation and derision. But Papa took them more literally.

He played to win, and he focused on winning with the same intensity that he concentrated on hunting, cooking, or telling his stories. He knew exactly what he wanted, and he pursued it with a singular purpose. He allowed nothing to stand in his way, not time or amusement or sympathy. The struggle riveted him, and he was focused and decisive, constantly aware that the outcome of his actions played a part, however small, in determining who he was. He was magnanimous in victory and gracious in defeat, and as soon as the game was over, he was relaxed and easy. But when he was playing, Papa was a formidable opponent.

After he had beaten me for a few hands, we stared across the garden, watching the freshly turned earth spatter beneath the drops. The rain magnified the stillness of that empty place, and the turn of each leaf, the spatter of each drop of rain, seemed infinite.

"The world globes itself in a drop of dew," Emerson wrote.

I really thought, in that moment, that I understood what had drawn Aha-no back to this place. Maybe what he saw here was not just the past, but also the future, in the shapeless and distant clouds, and in the heavy soil. Maybe he saw his future, and the future of his people, too. The stillness of this clearing, the way time seemed to stop here, was the point of perspective that made everything else a blur. But it emphasized for me how far away from home I was, sitting in this benevolent place with my estranged, adoptive father.

When the rain slowed and the patter against the mud began to abate, the sound died enough for us to speak. I wondered when we would start making our way home, but Papa seemed content to remain crouched beneath the outcrop. He was in a gregarious, almost giddy mood, suddenly talkative, a jumble of questions and statements. He *storied* about his childhood and about learning to hunt and to fight. He described his first tribal war, a mix of pride and wistfulness in his voice.

"Why are there tribal wars?" I asked.

He looked at me sideways, waiting for me to explain.

"Why do you fight?" I asked.

He shrugged. "To protect our women, land, pigs. To keep what is ours. We never start the fights," he assured me. "We do what we have to do. It's the same for you sometimes." I saw again in him that sense of inevitability that so baffled me.

"Things change, Papa. Time changes things," I said.

He furrowed his brow, and I knew that wouldn't make sense to him. Time was different here. It was like a constant breeze – noticeable, even comforting in its persistence, but never strong enough to alter anything. It was not a force or a dimension; it was more like a painting or a carving. He could examine it from a distance, notice its shapes and its contours, recognize the vision that it created and even admire himself in its reflection, all the while confident that it held no real power over him, would never touch him.

Whether he saw it or not, though, it did affect him, and he was changed by it. It had only been a few decades since this land had been discovered by the outside world. Since then, the Highlands had been turned upside down. These mountains now crawled with outsiders, the missionaries, mercenaries, and misfits. They all wanted something to take away.

But it was the perspective of the outsiders to think that they had "discovered" the Highlands, or to think that they could somehow change this place. They brought their cargo, their machines, and their God, and they planted themselves stubbornly in the middle of the rainforests until, like Shelly at the hotel bar, they no longer knew who they were. And all the while, the sun rose and set. The rain fell, crops grew, time passed.

We sat in silence for a moment, and then Papa slapped me on the shoulder.

"*Stori*," he requested, an expectant grin on his face.

I lowered my head and stared at the ground beneath me, my mind too preoccupied with its philosophical wanderings. Questions lingered, awaiting answers I didn't have.

I shrugged. "Can't think of anything, Papa." And his smile faded.

The hike back to the village was mostly downhill, and we kept a quicker pace than we had that morning, despite the weight we carried. My *bilum* chafed and bounced, and the muddy handle of the machete gritted against my palm. The rain continued, turning the path into a thick, orange mire. At one point, my feet slid from beneath me and I slammed to the mud, scattering the *kau kau* from my *bilum*. I pushed myself to my knees and knelt to catch my breath, my shoulders slumped, defeated.

Papa stopped and turned to gather the loose sweet potatoes. Then he stood before me and extended the broad, flat plane of his hand. For a moment, I stared at it, and then I wiped the mud from my hand and gripped his. He hoisted me upright, and we continued.

By the time we made it home, the day had drifted into the smoky skies above the mountains. Mama had somehow been foretold of our approach, and she waited at the gate, fists against her hips, clearly angry.

"Hello, Mama," I said.

"Late," was her only response. She noticed the mud caked to my arms and face, and thrust an accusing finger at Papa. "You," she shouted. "You pushed him too hard!" She glowered at him, and then came to me and put her hand on my cheek, wiping dried mud from my beard.

"My boy is tired," she said. "Come inside and rest. Your Papa will cook the dinner." She shot him another look, then turned and walked back toward the hut.

Papa and I climbed the gate, cautious to remain a few paces behind her.

Half an hour later, I sat on a log in the center of the *singsing* ground. Villagers came to greet me, shake my hand, and ask about our day. Tim sat beside me, shooing away the children as they tried to untie the laces on my boots or pull the hair on my legs. Francis offered me a stalk of sugar cane and sat on another log nearby. Inside our hut, Mama scolded Papa in a steady stream of *tok ples*, and I found the concern in her voice as comforting as the chirp of crickets. The clouds faded from the sky and darkness descended. A dozen people sat with me, telling jokes and stories.

The rain had been followed by a soft, gloaming breeze that swept the moisture from the air. No one bothered to light a fire, so we ate in darkness, subdued voices floating on the currents of dusk. Afterward, the women took the dishes. A couple of the men lit cigarettes of homegrown tobacco, and their embers cast glowing pinpoints in the darkness.

"*Nipi'e,*" someone said from the darkness, "*Stori.*"

I still couldn't make sense of all that had been tumbling through my

153

mind, and I didn't feel like I could push it away to tell carefree tales of a youth none of us would ever have again. Embarrassed by the attention, I only wanted to deflect it elsewhere, but I couldn't. I remained subject to my fear of disappointing them. "About what?" I asked.

"Anything," a voice responded.

So, I talked about my childhood, people I knew, things we did. I tried to draw things out, adding details, dramatic pauses. I alternated between speaking slowly and rapidly, and found my hands making grand gestures in the air, though no one could see them in the darkness. As soon as I had finished one story, they asked for another. I thought back to the ridiculous little adventures that had so absorbed my college friends and me as we sought the attention of women, tried to keep our cars running, or muddled through the dull ubiquity of classes.

I found myself gravitating toward funny stories, avoiding the sadness or seriousness that had weighed upon us all for so many days now. We talked late into the evening, our voices carrying across the serenity of the darkness, until the pauses between tales grew longer, and the words became increasingly interspersed with yawns and stretches.

Later, as I lay in the sleeping bag and the fatigue from the day's work seeped from my muscles, I felt a sense of serenity and ease I hadn't felt in days. But the echoes of what had happened still sounded, and their ghosts threw a shadow, like a *pentimento*, fragments of an old painting showing beneath a new one.

How do we live with the things we've done?

December 25, 1994 – Silent Night

Christmas arrived, almost unnoticed by us, amid the balmy succession of cloud, rain, and mud. To celebrate, the volunteers would have the opportunity call home. For most, it would be the first time we would speak to anyone in the States since we left, now more than a month ago.

With Christmas came the realization that our time in the villages would soon be coming to an end. The Papua New Guinean school year would begin in January and, in a few weeks, the volunteers would be leaving their villages and scattering to schools throughout the country. We had all begun to think about moving on.

In the conference room at Kefamo, someone had drawn a picture of a Christmas tree on the chalkboard. It was a crude sketch, little more than a green triangle with curled points at its edges, dotted with garish, exaggerated ornaments. A dozen boxes sat beneath it, adorned with fat ribbons and wide bows. The dazzling rays of the morning sun pierced the window louvers and filtered through the chalk dust that hung suspended in the air, obscuring the drawing, and filling the room with drowsy heat.

As we waited our turn to use the phone, we spoke with each other in disjointed conversations marked by prolonged silences. We paid little attention to one another, instead rehearsing what we would say in the ten minutes we had allotted each person to ensure everyone had a chance. An odd sense of reluctance, even dread, seemed to hang over us.

The letters I'd written to may family in the States may or may not have reached home yet, and in them I had only described the other volunteers and our training sessions, tried to give a sense of the mountains and the rainforest. I wrote of the embarrassment of bathing in front of an audience, and of the mythic beauty of the forested mountains. But I had said nothing about Aha-no's death or the murder of the woman. I wouldn't have known where to begin.

I had come to realize that I lost something during that week, something aside from my friendship with the old man. I didn't know then what it was, and even now the true essence of it eludes me, but I was sorry that it was gone, because I liked myself better when I had it. When I was still that person.

Maybe that's why I felt nervous about talking to my family. They would recognize that something was different, something was missing. I wouldn't know what to say if they asked about it. There would be no way of explaining it over the phone, as the line buzzed, and the minutes ticked.

At the rear of the room, a small booth contained an ancient cream-colored rotary phone, its finger holes encased in a thin layer of corrosion. Its side was pierced with a slot wide enough for the thick *kina* coins, and rust streaks crept to its rubber footing. At first glance, it seemed impossible that this pathetic little relic might somehow provide us with a link home. Its rounded base made it look animated, obese, obtuse.

When my turn came, I gripped the handle, dropped the coins into the slot and dialed the number of the house where my brothers and my sister had gathered to spend Christmas with my dad and stepmother. I heard a click as the line connected, and it briefly amazed me to hear ringing on the other end. My sister's voice answered, and I called her name.

Her voice raised an octave, and she shouted, "How are you?"

"Let me give you the number here," I said. It was the middle of the night in the States, but she promised to wake everyone and call right back, and we hung up.

The minutes seemed like hours as I waited for the return call, staring at the dormant telephone. It suddenly appeared as if its swollen belly had grown larger with the portents of bad news, some awful thing that had happened back home, about which I would only just now be learning. I envisioned my family dragging themselves out of bed, gathering and arguing over how to break the news.

What the hell was wrong with me? Where did this anxiety come from? Was it the stress of adjusting to this place? Was it the mefloquine, our anti-malaria medication, reputed to cause anxiety, depression, and vivid nightmares? I never used to be this neurotic. I left the booth and paced, never straying more than a few steps from the phone. The others wore curious and sympathetic gazes, watching me stride back and forth. Finally, the phone rang, and I lurched to grab it.

"Hello?" I bellowed.

"Christopher!" Dad said, and I was suddenly assailed by the duality of names I had come to recognize as my own. My host family had called me Nipi'e since the day I arrived, and all the volunteers had taken to referring to each other by village names, as well. I had an instantaneous gut reaction, wondering who Dad thought he was talking to.

"Dad," I said, my voice sheepish.

"How are you, boy?" he asked.

"Alright, I guess. You know, kind of tired." What a ridiculous thing to say.

There was a pause at the other end. The receiver buzzed with pops and scratches, and there was a delay as our voices traveled to the other side of the earth, disjoining the conversation. To combat the silences, both of us would begin talking at once, and then we would both stop to allow the other to speak, returning to awkward silence, until we had found a pathetic rhythm.

"Is there any snow there?" I yelled, and there was a pause.

"A bit," he said. "Not much. What's it like out there?" Pause.

"Well, there's no snow." Pause.

"No," he chuckled, "I wouldn't guess so." Pause.

"Sunny most days." I squinted at the rays that glared through the louvers and filtered through the chalk dust. "Doesn't seem feel like Christmas." Pause.

"Doesn't sound like Christmas," Dad agreed. Pause.

We went on like that, simple small talk separated by chasms of silence. The weather, family. I had only been gone a few weeks, and back home, nothing terrible had happened. In fact, nothing much had happened at all. Dad asked what it was like in my village, but I stuck to the basics: the mountains, the rainforest, the warped PMVs. Anything more would have been too much.

I spoke to my stepmother and tried to describe to her the plants and flowers that bloomed with such immensity and magnificence. But I didn't even know what any of them were called.

I talked to my brothers, one by one. We talked about football. The Packers were better this season than last, and in another year or two they might get to be really good. The same stuff we said every year when we didn't know what else to say. They asked similar questions to the ones Dad had asked, and I gave similar answers.

It's funny how distance softened the animosity of my bickering family.

My sister ended up on the phone again. "You sound tired," she said. "Take care of yourself. We're proud of you."

"Thanks," I said, and for the first and only time in the conversation, my voice cracked. I doubted she heard it, and was relieved. "I should go," I said. "A lot of people are waiting to use the phone."

"Sure," she agreed. "Dad's already calculating how much this call is going to cost."

"Take care," I said.

"I will," she promised. "Bye." Pause.

"Bye."

A deafening *click* terminated the line, and I replaced the phone on the cradle, where it once again sat, inert and pathetic. A few volunteers remained scattered around the conference room, murmuring quietly with one another. Conversation halted, and they lifted their heads as I passed. It felt like I should say something; everyone before me had finished their calls and left in a mysterious and heavy silence. But after a brief search for the right sentiment, I realized that there was nothing to say, and as the others had done before me, I left without a word.

January 11, 1995 – Medicine

"*Hamas longwe, Papa?*" I asked, "How far is it?" projecting my voice toward the unseen sounds of his hurried footfalls before me.

"*Em i no longwe tumas,*" he answered without breaking stride. "It's not very far."

I had asked the same question an hour before and received the same answer. Something told me there was no point in asking again. We had been walking since we finished dinner, heading west, chasing the falling sun as it disappeared before us to release the mountains from its warm embrace.

Gilbert was sick, with a high fever. He had barely eaten or nursed for days, and now he no longer had the energy to try. All day he'd been listless, silent, laying his head against Mama's shoulder, staring blankly at her neck.

Bacterial infections like typhoid and cholera were common in Highland villages, where families often lived beneath the same roof as their livestock, like Francis and his goat, and children slept alongside pigs and chickens on dirt floors. Drinking water came from the same muddy streams where villagers washed their clothes and bathed. We didn't know what was wrong with Gilbert, but we were worried.

Today, after he refused dinner, Mama and Papa decided to seek help. They would take him to a district medical station in the hills north of the village, near where the marriage ceremony of Mama's cousin had been. They tried to convince me to stay behind, but I insisted on coming with them, saying I wanted to do whatever I could to help. Without saying anything, I stuffed a wad of *kina* notes into my pocket, assuming it would be necessary for whatever treatment Gilbert might need, knowing my family wouldn't have it but would never ask me for help.

We wound along a narrow path through the fading light until nothing remained but darkness. Papa carried my flashlight, its beam too weak to illuminate much of anything in front of us. It only threw a meager beacon for me to follow, a pathetic splotch of light that staggered back and forth along the trail.

I knew the situation was serious. Given Papa's respect for the spirit world, marching into the night like this would have been unthinkable unless things were dire. Yet he walked quickly before me, without hesitation. A more immediate concern outweighed all others.

Mama and Papa spoke to each other in *tok ples*; stifled and hushed tones that crept blindly from the depths before me. I sensed their urgency, and their fear. I listened for sounds from Gilbert, hoping to hear a cough or a sigh, any sign of activity. Even his crying would have been reassuring, but he didn't make a sound.

I didn't want to think about the possibility of further tragedy falling upon my family and my village. There had been more than enough over the past few weeks. I was certain another one, especially this one, would break them. I had already decided if they couldn't help Gilbert at this jungle clinic, I'd insist we take him to a hospital in Goroka. If they couldn't help him there, I'd fly us to Port Moresby, and if Moresby wasn't good enough, I would put tickets to Australia on my credit card. I would do anything I could to keep this from happening.

We walked beneath the layered umbrella of the intertwined treetops. As immense as the forest seemed by day, it was infinite at night, and all things within it seemed mythical, coming from a place of enchantment and dream. An almost deafening chorus of crickets besieged us from amid the air itself, and fat drops of moisture fell from the leaves to measure our every step. A breeze fluttered through the woods and undergrowth, carrying the smells of woodsmoke and hibiscus.

We crossed a clearing where the canopy opened to expose the Southern Cross astride the shoulders of mountains, now silvered by brilliant starlight that seemed to belong to us alone. Beneath the constellations, wispy clouds draped across the ranges like blankets over the arched backs of sleeping children. Overcome by the vastness of it all, I suddenly felt pitifully small. I was struck again by the strangely familiar sense that I was falling through the damp air, as the mountains around me trembled, shrugged, and turned away.

When the beam of the flashlight finally stopped its unpredictable movements to shine steadily against the forest floor, I held where I was. I heard Mama in a hushed conversation with Papa. A third voice now spoke in the same whispered tones as my host parents, and I took a step closer.

The other voice belonged to a man, responding in short, terse notes to the more involved exhortations of my host parents. I could tell from the way he spoke he had a large wad of *buai* in his mouth, and he stopped to spit midway through.

The exchange didn't last long. I heard the stranger walk away, and then Mama and Papa whispering to each other again. They could have been two feet from me, or twenty. For all I knew I could have reached out my arm and touched them both. I still couldn't bring myself to say anything.

I heard a series of short, slinging sounds from the darkness, and an engine turned but failed to engage. I was suddenly thrown back to summer afternoons in Green Bay, heaving the starter cord on our dusty lawn mower, the smell of gasoline and wet grass, the Clash or David Bowie echoing from the garage. A generator roared to life, a throaty growl that jarred the soft serenity of the night, shattering the stillness like a chainsaw. And in an instant, a harsh and dazzling light flooded us. I shaded my eyes and turned aside until I adjusted to the illumination, and then I saw we were standing in a clearing before a small building.

It was a prefab, a kit house, perched six feet above the ground on metal stilts. A flight of wooden stairs led to a small porch at the front of the building, where a man stood barefoot, a *bilum* cap on his head, his beard streaked with gleaming *buai* spit. He beckoned to us, and we rushed up the stairs. Gilbert's eyes were unmoving and glossy. The man held the door and stared at me as I walked past him.

I would never get used to being stared at, in all my time in Papua New Guinea. It felt like they could see right through me, recognizing and observing all the doubts and flaws I tried so hard to hide.

Over the years, I found the weight of their stares more difficult, and sometimes infuriating, especially when I was tired, or homesick or stressed. Tonight, worried as we all were about Gilbert, it bothered me that this man, with a sick child who had been brought to him, still took the time to scrutinize me. I turned from him, retreated to a corner, and tried to make myself inconspicuous so he could focus his attention where it was needed.

The clinic consisted of two rooms, separated by a door of raw plywood. In the main room, illuminated by a bare bulb, two laminate counters ran along the walls, with cabinets above them and drawers below. Along one of the counters, a cutout made way for a sink that had never been installed. Instead, a rough opening bisected the Formica, revealing an empty space beneath it. The walls were painted blue-green, and a gecko scampered overhead, its footsteps echoing in the sparse room.

The man gestured to the child, and Mama lifted him from her shoulder and laid him gently on the counter. His face looked wan, and his head seemed too large for the rest of him. The man examined him, running his fingers along his neck, belly, and the edge of his ribcage. He poked and prodded, his spit-stained beard brushing just over his patient's face. Gilbert suffered with aplomb, lacking the strength to resist or complain.

The man turned his head to Mama and Papa to begin a staccato explanation. The expression on their faces was blank. They nodded mutely, staring at his mouth.

I saw, there in the harsh light of that bare bulb, as the generator roared outside the window, that Mama and Papa were consumed by a base, primal fear. Crippled by the helplessness that comes with unconditional love, they were impotent, left to the mercy of fate and this barefoot little man with a beard flecked with blood-red spit, in a jungle clinic in the middle of a rainforest.

He opened a drawer and withdrew a syringe. Then he began opening and closing cupboards, most of which were empty, working his way down the counter until he found what he was looking for: a small vial of clear liquid. He thrust the needle through the rubber stopper and drew back the plunger. Then he spoke to Mama, who turned Gilbert on his stomach and lowered his pants. Gilbert barely turned his head as the needle slid into his skin. When he was done, Mama lifted her son again, and he returned his head to the crook of her neck.

The man spoke some more and placed his hand on Gilbert's head. Mama and Papa nodded. Then he ushered us out the door and down the stairs, taking the opportunity to stare at me once again, and I suddenly felt ashamed of my previous impatience with him. As I passed him now, his eyes still searching me, I reached into my pocket for the money. He never gave an indication it was needed, though, and instead, I withdrew my empty hand and offered to shake his. At this, he smiled broadly and took my hand.

Then we were on our way again. We had barely left sight of the clinic before the generator switched off, dropping the forest back to its accustomed darkness.

The way back to the village, like most return trips, seemed shorter than the hike out had been. We were coming back to a place we knew, and we could hunker down there, and worry over Gilbert at home. While Mama and Papa had previously spoken in tense whispers, now there was only silence between them, the weak beam of the flashlight fumbling through the darkness in front of me.

We finally returned to the soft light of a campfire at Mari-eka, greeted by Francis and Tim and some of the others. They put their hands on Gilbert's back and sucked their teeth, trying to reassure each other everything would be ok. Mama and some of the women took Gilbert into the hut to put him to bed and continue to fuss over him, while Papa and I sat at the edge of the fire to listen half-heartedly to the stories being told there.

Papa stared at the embers, his face bloodless and slack. The flesh of his cheeks seemed to wither and melt in the heat of the fire, sliding to his jawline and hanging there. His shoulders hunched, arms resting on his knees, hands dangling limp, unmoving.

His hands were almost never motionless. They were always digging in the garden, cutting vegetables for dinner, illustrating *storis* on the tapestry of the air before him. But now they were empty, atrophied, and suddenly he looked his actual size to me, though he never had before.

Physically, he wasn't a big man, but his stature in my eyes had always been a reflection of his confidence, his authority, and his strength. These things made him bigger than he was— bigger than me, bigger than anyone I knew. They made him a giant.

But now, they had abandoned him. And in this moment, he was a helpless and frightened little man, vulnerable in a way I would never have thought possible. He had done all he could for his son, and he had to face how little that was. Now, there was nothing to do but wait, and that was a lot to ask of someone like him. He was a man who fought to keep the things that mattered to him. If there was something physical, tangible, knowable, that threatened his son, he would take it and throttle it, smother it, choke it into oblivion. With his hands, he could control it, transform it into something else, until it could no longer do any harm. But he had to touch it to know it.

This was something deeper. It wasn't even inside of Gilbert, not really. It was inside of Papa. This fear. And he couldn't reach it. He couldn't know it.

I remember the first time I saw my father cry. I was fourteen, and my parents were in the middle of their divorce. We sat in his tiny, depressing apartment, which seemed to have been purpose-built for divorcing men to while away court-sanctioned quality time with their kids. It was a mere three miles from the house he had bought when we moved to Green Bay, five years before. I don't remember what triggered it, just that he was trying to explain to my brother and me what was happening. But I remember watching him slump, watching his shoulders shake, his face contort, as his tears began to flow. I remember the way he seemed to shrink before my eyes.

There is an unavoidable moment in a boy's life, when for the first time he sees his father on the same level as he sees himself. It is as horrible and frightful as it is invigorating and affirming, because on some level, the child knows it is necessary, and he knows things will never be the same again, and his heart aches to have back that person who is infallible and unwavering and is the strongest person the child has ever known. But at the same time, the boy senses in the end this will be a good thing, because only afterward can he stop seeing his father as a figure and start

164

seeing him as a person, and from that point on, they can relate to one another from a place of actual understanding. When the time comes, they can be friends.

All this the boy knows instinctively, as it is happening. And yet all he wants is for it not to happen.

January 15, 1995 – Bilas

Gilbert got better; the way kids do. He woke up hungry the next morning, and within a few days he was running around as if nothing had happened. The ordeal of his illness melted away, and no one mentioned it again. The pattern of time and the passage of days in the village slipped back into routine, and I began looking beyond my time there, anticipating my two-year assignment teaching English in a district high school. In a couple of weeks I would be leaving the village, leaving my family.

As Barry had predicted, there were no repercussions to the death of the woman. No one from the provincial government or local police investigated, though they would certainly have heard about it.

I learned from Tim that warriors from the woman's houseline, seeking reparation, had come to Mari-eka one afternoon when I wasn't there. Tim thought it would please me to know that nobody from her village had denied the accusations against her. Their concern was that, as members of her tribe, they were entitled to compensation for her death. As far as Tim was concerned, her people had conceded her guilt. The negotiations were peaceable, with the only actual hostilities being the uprooting of some of the village gardens in a show of force.

In the end, the people of Mari-eka gave the warriors from her village a few *kina* and a couple of pigs, and the matter was settled. No one retrieved her remains. I don't even know where they left her remains.

I wonder how it would have made the woman feel, if she could have known of these arrangements; what it would have meant to her to know her life would be valued at no more than a few notes of currency and a couple head of livestock. Would she have taken offense? Or would she have accepted the summation, knowing it didn't matter?

The knowledge that her people never tried to proclaim her innocence only further confused the notion of what purpose it served. She seemed even more lonesome to me. In life, no one defended her; in death, no one mourned her. She had been so easily dismissed and forgotten.

It was simple fate that Aha-no had died when he did; it could just as easily have been weeks earlier, before the woman had followed us home from Soti's wedding. What would have happened then? The people of my village barely knew of her existence; would they still have found some way to blame her? Or would they have sought someone else? Another woman, whose intrinsic value to her society was dwindling? Were such considerations even part of the conscious decision-making process of who to blame?

If they hadn't killed her, how much longer would she have lived? How much longer would she have taken the meager products of her garden to the market to sit beside those same women, the soles of their bare feet coated in the clay mud of the Highland trails? Do women still go to that market today, and still laugh with the same abandon they did then? Do they know what happened there, all those years ago? I wonder if it might make life seem more tenuous to them, more precious. It could just as easily be any of them.

But it wasn't. It was her. And she no longer goes to the market, and those who do have neither the luxury nor the inclination to dwell on her memory. Whether or not the actions of my village were an affront to morality, or to anyone's god, or to the fabric of society, nothing relieves those women from the simple weight of their responsibilities. There are gardens to be tended, wood to be gathered, food to be prepared, children to be watched. The sun rises, the crops grow, the rain falls.

Two weeks into the new year, I was leaving Kefamo for my village when I passed Barry's office. He sat at his desk with sandaled feet on the desktop, reading an Australian newspaper. I knocked, and he looked over the paper and pushed up his glasses.

"Do you have a second?" I asked, and he nodded and put the paper down. "We're heading out soon, and I just wanted to say thanks for everything. I appreciate it."

He shrugged his shoulders and laced his hands behind his head, as I had seen him do so many times. "Hopefully," he said, "you guys have learned a few things that'll help you down the road. The cycle turns fast here – birth, growth, death, rebirth. When you go to your school, it will all be going down around you. What matters is that you are able to find yourself in the middle of it."

"It's funny, you know?" I said. "For all this time in the village, all the awkwardness, all the hardships, I thought a lot about leaving. I pictured it – being finished. Now it's almost here, right in front of me, and I can't even envision it. I don't know how I'm going to leave."

He just grinned his Cheshire cat grin and said, "Maybe that's a sign it's time to go." There was a certain order to that – it made sense to Barry.

I sometimes wonder – if I had never left that village, if for some reason I had stayed and I was still there today, whom would I have become? In many ways, I think I'd be closer to the person I was when I arrived, mostly because that's where I left him. Some part of me thinks he's still there, and I miss him very much.

I doubt if I were to go looking for him, that I'd be able to find him. I know he's still there, though. He's frozen in time, unchanged, and I am drawn to a memory of him, just the as Aha-no was drawn to the garden where Papa and I harvested sweet potatoes. Because in those moments, in those fragments, somehow both fleeting and eternal, we can control time instead of it controlling us. Past, present, and future become one, and we can halt the movement and progression of the continuum. We can replay the moment, relive it, turn it over and over again, examine its intricacy, find its patterns and networks, connect that instant to others that passed before and after. We can find or instill in it a beauty we may not have seen before, and we can revel in our accomplishments and wax poetic about what we might have been.

And when we put it back, we are secure in the knowledge it will be just where we left it, just as we left it, for the next time we need it again.

* * *

The village held a feast to observe my approaching departure. It was a reflection on my time there, a chance to begin saying goodbye. They held another *mumu*, like the one at Soti's wedding. They slaughtered a pig, and though I didn't see it butchered, the gray skin apparent in the cuts of meat gave me the sinking feeling it was Wilbur.

Inside our hut, Papa and Francis prepared my *bilas*, ceremonial decoration. They gathered the items necessary to decorate me in the ancient traditions of the Highlands, and when everything was ready, they motioned for me to join them.

They had assembled a collection of leaves, one with a small mound of mud in it, another with a pile of berries, and two more with dollops of thick paint. Next to these, draped over a stone, were several strands of beads, another of cowry shells, and a few fur pelts. There were feathers, *tanget* leaves, bones, and a polished bow with a dozen arrows. Papa stood beside the collection, stripping leaves from a branch and piling them atop the stone. He gestured at the log stone near the hearth, my accustomed spot, and I sat and waited.

"Take off your shirt," Papa said, "and your boots."

Francis and his sons began dipping flowers into the mud and pressing the petals against my leg, leaving perfect renderings against my skin. They set about covering my legs, chest, and arms with the tiny mud flowers. One of the kids took my hand and, with great care, painted a series of narrow triangles, each originating at my wrist and tapering above each knuckle. He repeated the process on my other hand.

Francis took the strings of beads and cowry shells and tied them around my waist. He wrapped an intricately carved rattan band around each of my upper arms. Then he took handfuls of leaves, deep green on top and maroon underneath, and tucked them into the armbands.

He hung two *cuscus* pelts around my neck, one against my chest and the other on my back. There were also two smaller pelts, which he fastened around my wrists. He tucked small bones into these.

"These bones come from the bird we call *nipi'e*," he said, and he pointed at me, "your namesake. They are for courage."

Into the bands around my upper arms he tucked some of the larger bones. "These come from the *cuscus*," he said. "They are for cunning, and for patience."

Finally, he took the largest bones and tucked them into the band at my waist. "These," he told me, "are bones of our ancestors. They are for wisdom." At that, he stepped back with his children, and gave me a moment to gaze at the bones tucked at my waist. Human bones: from the ancestors of this village. There was something soothing about their feel, solid and unyielding, against my waist.

Francis motioned for me to stand, and as I did, one of the boys came forward with his arms full of *tanget* leaves. Each of the boys took a few and circled me, tucking the leaves into the belt of cowry shells, creating a leaf skirt.

Now Francis stood before me, his sons by his side. He dipped his index finger into the black paint, pressed it against my left temple and dragged it down my forehead to the bridge of my nose. He traced a line around my left eye and across my cheek, until it reached the edge of my beard. He added a crescent that followed my lower eyelid from the bridge of my nose to my temple. Then he followed the same pattern on the right side.

Now he began applying the white paint, following the same lines, shadowing the black. Then he began with the yellow, filling the patches that had not been covered. Both cheeks, below the eyes and above my beard, were now bright yellow, bordered by white and black lines, with a triangle of yellow down my forehead to a widow's peak. Francis wiped his hands and coated my beard with mud.

Papa stood at the opposite end of the fire and cast a critical eye. He approached me, carrying a *bilum* cap in his hand. He gestured for me to sit again, and he pulled the cap as far over the crown of my head as he could, so it sat tight against my scalp.

He took two bundles of brightly colored bird feathers, three inches long. They were fiery reds and yellows, explosive colors that seemed to generate their own light in the dimness of the hut. He tucked the shorter feathers under the skullcap, one at each temple, so they hung at either side of my head, down to the edge of my jaw. The yellow of the feathers matched the yellow paint below my eyes.

Papa retreated to the dark recesses of the hut, and the kids shifted their feet restlessly. Francis shushed them, and for once they did as he told them. Papa returned carrying the crowning feature of the *bilas*: three more feathers. Two were alike, wide and thick, maybe eight or ten inches long, but the other was nearly three feet long, and several inches wide. The quill was curved and drooped under its own weight. Papa held the feathers reverently before him.

"These come from a bird that is very difficult to hunt," he said, as he affixed the feathers into the skullcap, extending them straight above my head.

The feathers came from a black sicklebill, a rarebird of paradise found only in the Highlands. More than a year later, beneath the low clouds of a gray and rainy day, I would see in flight while I hiked near the school where I taught.

It would be the only time I ever saw one in the wild. It had a long, gracefully curved beak jutting from a tiny crown. Its compact breast and mantle supported a wingspan that looked too narrow to keep it aloft. Its most prominent features were its long tail feathers, many times the length of its body, which trailed behind it like an anchor.

In a way, this strange bird, so at odds with its own physique, came to strike me as a perfect emblem of the place itself. I could think of nothing more Papua New Guinean than what I saw that day. I remember watching this beautiful, pitiful creature struggle against its awkwardness, against itself, saddled with the enormity and the cumbersomeness of its own raw magnificence, as it made its resolute journey across clouded and unhelpful skies. Watching it fly was an exercise in the profound frustration of empathy, but there was also an implicit elegance in its unselfconscious determination.

"These birds are very clever," Papa continued, "this is why our warriors wear their feathers."

"The feathers make the warriors clever?" I asked.

He shook his head. "*Bilas* does not make a man clever. But it shows what he is like inside, helps him to find those things in himself. It shows that we are together. Our *lain*, our tribe, matters more than anything. This *bilas*," he said, gesturing at the decorations that now covered my entire body, "is who we are. And so now we decorate you, so that when you leave this place, you will remember where you come from." He held up a finger and looked me in the eye. "So you won't forget."

Over Papa's shoulder, Francis clutched his children in the dim light. They studied my face paint, the fur pelts, and the head dress, fussing over the details. After consulting with Francis, Papa announced that I was ready.

"Now you will come outside, and show your family," he said.

I paused. "Could I be alone for a minute first?"

Papa nodded and he and Francis herded the kids out the door. "When you are ready," he said.

Outside, people had gathered, watching and waiting. Several craned their necks to catch a glimpse through the door, but Papa closed it behind him.

I retreated to the rear of the hut, careful with the feathers that bobbed several feet above my head. I located my shaving mirror, disused now for weeks, and I returned to the fire and crouched there to capture its light. The flames feinted and leapt, sometimes illuminating my face, others plunging it into darkness, but the disjointed instances came together enough for me to assemble an image. I marveled at what Papa and Francis and the kids had done, the transformation they had brought about. I barely recognized myself.

I thought about the significance of this gesture and wondered if it was the emblem of acceptance that I wanted it to be. I knew I wasn't one of them – I was still an oddity, a spectacle. But I was coming to realize that their approval of me was never based on me becoming one of them. It was contingent on something else.

They had watched me, assessed me, even scrutinized me, and they had always seen me for the person I was. And yet, they had concluded that, despite our differences, I was worthy of their acceptance. Not as a Westerner, or as a volunteer, or a traveler, a teacher. Not as "the other." They merely received and embraced me as myself. And as I sat there, listening to the fire murmur beside me, feeling the paint drying on my face and the mud hardening in my beard, I realized they knew who I was, beneath the paint and the mud, beneath even my pale skin. They had known all along, and they *wanted* me to be there. And though I was not one of them, and never would be, I felt a sense of belonging as great as any I had ever felt before.

Yet this revelation didn't bring the feeling of euphoria I had expected.

172

Instead, it was tinged with a sense of melancholy, as I listened to the expectant crowd that stood gathered outside our hut. My perception of my adoptive family had evolved so much. I had been forced to acknowledge what I didn't want to see: that they were flawed people, just as I was.

Now, I see the irony of that recognition. Throughout my time in the village, I had been afraid I would let them down by not being what they expected me to be, that they would see me as insecure, ambiguous, unreliable, and afraid. It had never occurred to me that *they* might not be what *I* expected them to be – that they struggled with uncertainty, and that they could act selfishly, compelled solely by fear. I wasn't ready to discover this about them. I hadn't known what to do with it.

They made their way in a world in which little was given to them, and what they had could easily be taken away. They knew how fleeting their existence could be; they saw the cycles of it play out before them every day. They didn't have the musings of philosophers and theologians from which to draw their framework of morality, so they looked no further than the rainforests that surrounded them.

But when the outside world came to embrace and engulf them, the missionaries, mercenaries and misfits trampling through the forests to nearly suffocate its inhabitants, the people of the villages looked to their past to find a sense of equilibrium. They sought comfort in the familiar, just as the other volunteers and I did when we felt overwhelmed by the exoticism of their world. They drew upon a time when things made sense to them. They acknowledged an obligation to thousands of years of cultural and spiritual heritage.

I came to see that I had not been embraced by the simple and childlike natives I had expected. Instead, they were complicated, imperfect people, tarnished by the fundamental failings that mar us all. My expectations of them were no more realistic than theirs had been of me before they met me.

My acknowledgement of their flaws and vulnerabilities may have drawn me closer to my host family, and made me more aware of the composition of the society in which I would spend the next two years. But did it mean I'd made it through the looking glass to see the world as they saw it, through their eyes? Or did I merely feel the empathy of the poet, so moved by the attachment I felt that I mistook it for understanding?

I finally stood and tossed the mirror back into my duffel. Then I opened the door and stepped into the sunlight to stand amid my family.

A cheer arose from the crowd, a mixture of whoops and shouts. I heard my name chanted, from all sides around me. I heard the same deep wailing the women had made on the day that I arrived. The villagers pressed forward, and once again I felt hands running across my arms and my chest, pulling at my shoulders, hugging my legs.

I moved to the center of the *singsing* ground and the crowd swarmed with me. Along the edge, I saw that some of the old women had painted their faces, smearing orange mud on their cheeks and foreheads, an expression of mourning at my imminent departure. They wailed and danced along the edge of the crowd, their faces lifted to the sky, hands flinging at their sides.

I felt a hand on my arm and saw Tim beside me. "That is a traditional dance," he said, and then he gestured with his chin. "Go on, do it just like they are."

The crowd backed away from me, and the women continued to dance as if oblivious to my indecision. I set aside my self-consciousness, and I went at it with all the enthusiasm I had. I got in line behind them, jogged the same path around the crowd as they had taken, casting my eyes upward and shaking my hands at my sides. The crowd cheered, and many fell into line behind me, stomping, shaking, and chanting.

There was something liberating in the openness of the dance, as more and more of the villagers joined our circle. Soon, everyone was dancing, and we fell into a syncopated rhythm. Our bare feet stomped harder and harder on the clay surface, and our shouts and chants became louder. Papa handed me the bow and arrows, and I tramped along the outside of the circle, gesturing with the weapons toward the ground and at the sky. The crowd grew louder, faster, building to a crescendo of one long, steady, and cathartic shout, after which everyone collapsed. They gathered around me again, laughing, shaking my hand, slapping my shoulder, and I held the bow and arrows above my head and unleashed a whoop. Others joined in, building to another crescendo, more laughs, more pats on the back.

174

We threaded through the village in a long and winding line. We edged the fire pit where we had sat and told our stories. We skirted the garden plots, teeming with yams, taro, pumpkin greens, and banana trees. We passed the hut where the women had been held captive, its door now ajar, only darkness within. I stared as we passed, feeling as if the silent place returned my gaze with an accusatory one if its own.

My sense of despondency resurfaced. This rite of passage, like any other, was bittersweet.

We circled the village and hopped the gate, passing the trail that led to the waterfall where I washed. We crossed the bridge and descended the main path, sweeping through neighboring villages. People gathered outside their huts and along the edges of their gardens to witness the bizarre spectacle of a white man in *bilas*. But our reception was the same everywhere we went: calls, whoops, and pats on the back. More joined us, and the crowd grew. Soon, a hundred people followed us – men, women and children marching and chanting in the same rhythm.

Mama approached me as I led the crowd back into the village. She took me by the shoulder and turned me toward the people behind me. "Look at your family one more time before you remove your *bilas*," she said. "They are here for you. Remember always that your family is here for you."

I looked at the crowd, their faces gleaming in sweat, chests heaving from their exertions, and I was overcome by the closeness I felt to them. I waved my hand high in the air, and they cheered. I turned to Mama and I promised her, "I won't forget."

She nodded, and said, "Now go and wash."

Inside the hut, I removed the headdress, carefully lining the feathers alongside one another in the dim recesses. Papa entered the hut as I wiped the paint and mud from my face and beard, and he began organizing the feathers and shells and skins to be stored.

"Lots of people," he said. "A good day."

I nodded. "I'm happy to see them," I said.

"You must thank them for being here," he said, "for coming to celebrate."

He was right; I needed to show my appreciation. But I had no idea what to say.

"Now?" I asked.

He nodded, and then, sensing my unease, he smiled. "*Bai mi tok pastaim,*" he said. "I'll speak first."

We emerged to find even more people, standing shoulder to shoulder in our village. They were everywhere, young and old, men and women, children large and small laughing and racing through the huts and gardens. All were full of energy and enthusiasm, but as soon as Papa called, they gathered around us. He stood on a tree stump next to our hut and addressed them with accustomed authority.

"Many people have come today," he began, "We are happy you are with us. Plenty of food is here, and everyone will eat well. But first, I would like to say something about why we are here." He looked down at me, then back to the crowd. "Some time ago, men came to this village, to talk to Aha-no." The crowd hushed at the mention of the old man. "They asked if we would like to have a white man come and stay in the village. This man would be new to our land. He would not know of our *tok* or our *pasin*. He would come here to learn from us. He would be like a child. We would take care of him, feed him, watch him, and teach him. A great responsibility. Aha-no asked me if I could keep this man in my house, with my family. And I said yes."

"Then," Papa continued, "he came." He put his hand on my shoulder. "And he was like a child. A boy. He couldn't even go to the river to wash without us watching him, making sure he was okay." A murmur of laughter worked its way through the group.

"But he was *our* boy," he said, "our son. And we watched him learn. We watched him grow. Now he is grown, and it is time for him to leave us. He will go and teach children in their school." He paused again. "We have done what we could for him. Today we say goodbye, wish him well and remind him that he must not forget us, because we are his family. I want to say thank you to all of you, for coming here to help us to celebrate. And I want to say thank you to my son, Nipi'e, for giving himself to my village and my people."

The crowd applauded, and Papa stepped down and gestured at the stump. I took his place and faced the crowd, a sea of expectant and encouraging

176

faces. They waited as I took a breath and chose my words. My speech was halting, my Pidgin failing me just when I needed it most. But I forged ahead, determined to say what I could.

"When I came to this village," I began, "I was afraid. Afraid that it would be difficult for me to be in this place, live with the people here, and let them help me and take care of me. This wasn't easy for me to do." I paused again. The crowd smiled, and nodded, and I swallowed, fighting nerves and emotion.

"I've never seen a place like this before," I said. "There is a beauty in this land that I cannot describe in your language, or in mine. Not just the mountains and the trees and the rivers, but in the *pasin* of this place, and the people that belong to it." I stopped, running out of words again.

"When I came here, I thought, I will learn the language, learn about the culture, and then I will go. But my time here was more than that. The people talked about being my family. These weren't just words to them. They treated me like a son, took care of me like a son, and loved me like a son. They gave me more than I could give back. All I can say is thank you, to my Papa, and my Mama, and to all of you. Thank you for what you have done for me. I promise I will not forget this place. I will not forget you."

I stepped down from the stump, knowing my words had been inadequate, that I had not expressed what I meant, could not possibly have described the vastness of what I felt. But they applauded and cheered. The words weren't there, but they were able to read me, like they always did. The blood rushed to my face, and I lowered my head, awed by the joy and the sadness, relief and anxiety, accomplishment, and loss.

Tim squeezed through the crowd to shake my hand. "It was good, what you said. It made them happy."

"I didn't say enough," I said.

He shook his head. "They understand," he assured me.

Soon, the food was ready. The women cut slabs of pork and pieces of sweet potato, wrapping them in leaves and handing them to guests. There was barely enough for everyone.

I walked among the crowd, fluctuating between humbled gratitude and the familiar sense that I didn't deserve their esteem. This ceremony symbolized the end of my time in the village, and so it was time for me to assess what I did there, and the only conclusion I would allow myself to draw was that I hadn't done enough. I hadn't lived up to what they deserved from me, hadn't done for them all I could have. I hadn't helped them understand the changing world that encroached ever closer upon them. I couldn't save them, just as I couldn't save her.

They told me, time and again, by word and by look, that it was ok, but I couldn't accept it, couldn't allow myself to be in the moment and enjoy it. Burdened with my failures, I sat and spoke with the people of my village, crouched on the packed clay of the *singsing* ground, and our conversations were seldom more than brief exchanges as the emotion overcame me time and again.

"Your Mama and your Papa will miss you," said one.

"I'll miss them too," I said. "I will miss my village."

"Be careful when you go to your new place," said another. "Some people, they are savages, and want only to fight."

"I'll be careful," I said.

"You must not forget your family here," someone insisted.

"I won't forget," I promised.

A long day was ending. As the sun set and the sky faded to a pinkish hue, I worked with the darkened figures to build a huge, roaring fire. Others gathered, and we danced again, though less frenetically than we had in the light of day. We told stories as we had on so many evenings before, and everyone talked about our time together.

Papa told of the day he and Francis had found me in the pouring rain, wearing Mike's oversized poncho and flinging mud with a dozen children. He talked proudly about our recent trip to the garden, how well I had handled the long hike, how hard we'd worked there. Tim told about a hike we had taken one day to the top of the mountain called *Gusa-kave*, and the fruitless search we had conducted there to find my namesake bird. Francis told about driving me to rugby matches, eating scones and drinking sodas from glass bottles.

As they spoke, Mama sat beside me, a hand on my shoulder, running her fingers through my hair. "*Pikinini bilong mi gat gras olsem Rambo*," she said. "My child has hair like Rambo," and everyone laughed.

Someone else, whom I didn't recognize, told a story about watching from afar on an early morning as I made my way down the trail. The path was muddy and slick, and I had slipped at a steep part and slid down the hill. After coming to a stop, I had stood, wiped off my shirt and my shorts, and adjusted my *bilum*. Seeing the spectator at the top of the hill, I had waved and continued down the trail. Everyone laughed, and the teller asked if I remembered the morning I fell on the trail.

I shook my head, "I fall on the trail *every* morning." And we laughed some more.

The stories continued as the guests came and went, until finally I apologized and told everyone I had to sleep. They stood with me, shaking my hand and patting my back as I made my way to the hut. At the door, I turned and spoke.

"I know that I owe something to my family that I can never pay back," I said. "But I promise I will try."

They waved, and wished me a good night, and I ducked through the doorway.

January 18, 1995 – Goodbye

I had come to know and admire the way the people of the Highlands greeted the morning. The transition from sleep to wakefulness, like the passage from dark to light, was a deliberate, almost immeasurable journey. The dawn of a new day came in stages, as the stillness of night gave way to dripping moisture, droning insects, and fluttering whispers of the cooking fires.

The pressure of one day was seldom much greater or lesser than that of the day before, or the one that would follow. The Highlanders knew each day meant working in the gardens, beneath a relentless sun or driving rain, or hauling leaking water buckets up steep hillsides. But they knew too that rising in the morning and preparing for the day's labor was as much a part of their existence as sitting around the fire telling stories in the cool evening breeze, and so they applied no less enthusiasm to one than to the other.

There was a calmness in the way they drifted into their days, an acceptance of the continuity of being, that I envied. I have always sought to emulate the serenity I saw there, but I have never captured the self-possession so evident in the people of my village.

When I awoke on my last morning in Mari-eka, a dull ache gnawed at the pit of my stomach. The day had come.

Mama had a kettle on for the morning tea. I pulled on a shirt, stepped to the edge of the fire, and crouched there, staring into the flames.

The edges of her mouth curled into a quivering smile, but her eyes were darkened with sorrow. I almost couldn't face her, sensing her sadness, knowing I was the cause of it, and I felt a twinge of absurd anger, wondering why we worked so hard to create this sense of family, only to take it away.

I wanted to reassure her, make her see this wasn't a tragedy: that now her life could go back to normal. She would no longer be saddled with the responsibility of my well-being. Everything was okay; this was how it was supposed to be. But no words came, so instead I returned her gaze, the only sounds coming from the cooking fire as it splintered and sighed.

The silence broke as Gilbert began to cry. Mama went to retrieve him, and I took the opportunity to gather my things.

There wasn't much left to pack. I had given away my flashlight, my shaving mirror, the hurricane lamp, and many of my clothes, but I was methodical and meticulous in arranging what remained, because it gave me something to do. I clung to the simple comfort of a concrete task while I waited for the truck that would take me from this place. I cocked my head and sought the sound of its approach, eager for it and dreading it at the same time.

Mama handed me a cup of tea, and I emerged from the hut into the dazzling rays of the early sun. The heat of day was descending, but a light wind still emerged from beneath the long shadows of morning to wander along the valley and drape across the village with reassuring calmness.

Papa and Francis sat cross-legged beneath a casuarina tree. They seemed determined not to dwell on the sadness of the day, and I resolved I wouldn't, either. We would talk and tell our stories the way we always did, savoring the remainder of our time together.

I sat beside them, and we began our ritual of shared experiences. Francis talked about trips to town in his obstinate truck, and about the time a policeman chased us, and we left him flailing in the mud. Papa talked about hikes in the woods, working in the garden, and about Stanis, a man we met at a rugby match who offered me his niece to keep me warm at night, and they had a hearty laugh. We placed my *bilum* in the center, and took turns flipping cards into it. Wiling away the moments.

Drifting like sprites from the streambed came the voices of women, infused with an implicit joy, a light and easy laughter, as they beat clothes against the stones. They called to each other rapidly, with an urgency propelled by the intimacy of family and the certainty of its companion-ship. They chattered in *tok ples* and fell to fits of laughter, the laundry forgotten in an instant.

A group of small boys, with tufted hair sprouting from their heads and thick mucus creeping from their nostrils, raced around the backs of the huts, chasing a rat that had wandered into their path. They shouted with absolute and focused delight as they shoved each other aside in pursuit of their prey. They were naked, and they ran without a trace of timidity or self-consciousness. The rat darted into the undergrowth, and the kids continued the chase, disappearing into the rainforest.

Visitors came and went, as they had the night before, and we mostly avoided the topic of my departure. If someone mentioned it, our smiles faded, and we lapsed into an uncomfortable silence until one of us turned the subject elsewhere. We shared a tacit agreement that it should not be spoken of.

While we retold our tales and threw the cards, we waited for this moment to pass, and we remembered the moments that had passed before it. I told each story with the same enthusiasm, threw each card with the same eagerness, but a part of me labored over the interminable passage of minutes, wanting it to be over, wanting to be gone. Not wanting to say goodbye, just wanting it to be said.

Finally, in the early afternoon, as the sun held high overhead and the initial clouds of an eventual rain crept slowly over the eternal mountain ranges, we heard the Land Cruiser labor up the hill and lurch across the bridge. The engine stopped, the door opened, and Sonny appeared, his *bilum* cap resting at its familiar angle, even as he leaned against the village gate and tilted his head to the sky, searching for the coming rain.

Papa stared at Sonny and said, "It's time." I nodded and stood, not knowing where to look or what to say. I walked back to the hut to retrieve my things.

Inside, Mama tended the fire and rocked Gilbert on her knee. "It's time for me to go, Mama," I said. She stood as I took my bag. I turned to face her and then embraced her and Gilbert.

Pidgin, like the various forms of *tok ples* used throughout the Highlands, has no commensurate word for 'goodbye.' The sentiment is too final, and Papua New Guineans detest finality. They don't believe in endings. When bidding farewell, Papua New Guineans say, "*Lukim yu bihain*," which means, "I will see you again," and the finality, even if certain, is never acknowledged.

I assured Mama I would see her again, even as I wondered if I would. She may have wondered the same thing, but faithful to the proscriptions of her society, she gave no indication, and I was grateful.

"Kiss your brother," she told me, and I obediently leaned over to kiss Gilbert on the forehead. For once, he didn't cry. "And when you're in your place, wherever you go, remember your family here."

I still remember with absolute clarity the expression on her face when she said that. Smiling and crying at the same time. How is that possible? She felt the sadness of my departure, and she understood the significance of me moving on. She understood the joy and the sorrow, and she embraced them both, and so she smiled a genuine smile through her tears, and she made an uncharacteristically grand, sweeping gesture with her hand as she said "wherever you go," and I knew she didn't just mean my school or Moresby or any other parts of her country I saw, but she meant the world over. She wanted me to remember I had a family here. And I could only nod through tears of my own.

Then, I turned and left the hut.

As I passed through the village, people gathered once more to walk those last few steps with me. Papa and Francis stood with Sonny, leaning against the hood of the Land Cruiser, watching the sky, and chatting.

I hefted my duffel up to my shoulder and climbed to the top of the gate. I remembered my arrival, straddling that split rail fence, one foot in my past, the other in my future. I remembered thinking at the time about all the things that lay before me then. Were they all behind me now? This feeling, this mix of accomplishment and of remorse, of invigoration and exhaustion, expectation, and uncertainty: is this wisdom, or just what it is to be?

I climbed down to say more goodbyes. Francis approached me, looking deflated without his accustomed smile. We shook hands, then embraced, and he backed away to sit on a rocky outcrop at the edge of the trail. His children gathered around him, surrounded and engulfed him. They clung to his arms, his legs, his round belly. One even stood behind him to wrap his arms around his father's head. He looked out from within this cocoon, and I saw his smile return, and I was relieved. It didn't feel right to see my uncle so serious.

Tim jogged up the trail to meet me and arrived out of breath. "Nip'ie," he said. "I am sorry to see you go. But I will see you again, brother. I will come and visit you at your school. Maybe someday I will come and see you in your country!"

"I'd like that," I told him, and we hugged. He smiled, then turned and walked away, every step leaving a clear imprint of his bare feet in the soft mud.

Papa watched the goodbyes silently, his face and his movements controlled, serene and reassuring. I lowered my head for a moment, and then looked at him.

"Papa," I said. "It's time for me to go."

He nodded, and then my Papa surprised me one last time.

His face twitched for an instant, his chest struggled to draw a breath, and he began to cry. Like the spontaneous appearance of an afternoon rain, there was no forewarning. Instead, in an instant he threw his arms around me and collapsed into loud, heaving sobs. He cried against me as the breeze crept through the village and clouds encroached upon the placid expanse of cerulean sky. He pressed the side of his face to my chest, and the warmth of his tears seeped through my shirt. His shoulders trembled, his breath came in short gasps, and he unashamedly poured out his sadness before the entire village.

Mama stood at the edge of the gate, and Gilbert, seeing his father cry, whimpered also. He plugged his fingers into his mouth and muffled his sobs into the creases of his tiny hand.

I held my arms around Papa. "*Mi sori tumas, Papa, long lusim famili bilong mi,*" I said. "I'm very sorry to leave my family, Papa."

After a few moments, it was over, and he was finished. He stepped away from me, his dark eyes watching from above his thick beard. He regained his composure as quickly as he had relinquished it.

"*Lukautim gut long nupela ples,*" he said. "Be careful in your new place."

I nodded, climbed into the Land Cruiser and gently pulled the door shut.

The engine groaned and we began to pull away, approaching the bridge, and I turned to take a last look at my village. Most of the villagers stood in their place, watching us go, though many of the kids had mercifully lost interest and begun chasing each other over the path and under the gate.

I stared out the window of the Land Cruiser, and I watched the rainforest crawl past us as we made our way down the trail for the last time.

Smoky clouds continued creeping across the horizon, diminishing the sunlight that glinted from the windshield. A gentle tapping began against the roof.

It was beginning to rain.

Today – Aftermath

I used to think that, when my two years in Papua New Guinea were done, I would simply leave it behind; that it would diminish in my memory to become just another place I had been. I knew pieces of it would remain with me, but I thought time would eventually dismantle those pieces and carry them away, the way the ants carried away the cockroach on the bamboo floor of our hut on that cloudy morning all those years ago.

Instead, the opposite happened. The bits and fragments of my time there have come together in my consciousness more completely than they did when I was there, and in many ways, I feel closer to that place now than I did the day I left. All that has transpired since my time in the village seems only to have brought me back there. I rarely go longer than a few weeks without dreaming about it, dreaming about being back there.

I spent two years in Papua New Guinea after my time in the village. But I never returned to Mari-eka, and I never saw my host family again.

For the first year after leaving the village, I taught in a high school 7,000 feet up in the western shadows of Mt. Giluwe, in the Southern Highlands. After local conflicts and tribal wars spilled onto the school grounds, I was transferred for my second year to the island of New Britain, to a school located at the edge of an overgrown and derelict copra plantation that had once been among the remotest outposts of the Japanese Empire during World War II. The Japanese had abandoned it to the whine of mosquitoes and the screech of parakeets, much as I found it fifty years later.

In both schools, I taught English literature and grammar to students who lived in barracks-style dormitories, where they feverishly prepared for the matriculation exams that determined their fate. Those who scored in the highest percentiles won the right to continue in school, while anything less than a stellar performance meant the end of an academic career. The kids who failed had virtually no chance of finding a job in the city, and even those who finished high school found few spots in the country's only university, and even fewer chances to study abroad. For most Papua New Guinean students, their education would be brief, and it was a near certainty that when it was over, they would make their way back to the villages that had sent them with such high hopes.

The kids I taught came from subsistence farming villages like Mari-eka, a fact I never allowed myself to forget, and it profoundly influenced the way I treated them. I tried, always, to show the respect, the admiration and the pride I had learned in my time in my village. They deserved nothing less from me.

Spending time with my students there was one of the great privileges of my life. Their optimism and resilience in the face of abject poverty, diminishing opportunity and occasional brutality never ceased to amaze me. They were respectful, generous, eager, and fun. And they ruined me for teaching. I doubt I could ever again have found students who could duplicate their implicit joy and unshakable hope, products of the villages from which they had come and the families that raised them.

When my time in Papua New Guinea was done, I went back to Green Bay, because I didn't know where else to go. I tried to disappear into another cold, gray winter, shoveling snow from the driveway of my mother's house, suffocating in my down coat, like the one Elvis wore as he stumbled drunk around Mari-eka.

I remember, a few days after I returned, walking through a grocery store the size of an airplane hangar, with vents descending from high ceilings to circulate the hot, dry air that barely kept the outside chill at bay. I remember running my hands along the endless aisles of shrink-wrapped deli meats, microwave dinners and frozen pizzas, all the while recalling the splintered shelves of scarcely-provisioned Highland trade stores, the scattered rows of tinned fish, rubber sandals and kerosene lanterns draped in dust. I remember sitting in a darkened bar with high school friends, cowed by

187

loud music, flashing lights and TV screens of frenetic images, as I yearned for a stubby of lukewarm SP beside the pool at the Bird of Paradise hotel.

In my time abroad, the notion of "home" had been a beacon; a point of reference for all I observed, a place of comfort and certainty while I drifted in a sea of exotic faces, unfamiliar languages, strange food, scorching sun and torrential rain. "Home" was also the place to which I would return when my time was over, and so the shock of my arrival was all the more acute when I found that "home" wasn't what I remembered. Even the most familiar things – my old bedroom with its little twin bed and the unfinished desk my dad had made – failed to impart to me the familiarity I needed.

My repatriation was more disconcerting than my departure had been. My home hadn't changed in any noticeable way in the time I was gone, yet what I found wasn't what I had left behind. My time away suddenly seemed nothing more than a *wokabout*, a *spin tasol*, leading me back to back where I had begun. I had escaped this place once before, but now it wouldn't allow me back. I tried to push away my time in Papua New Guinea and focus on the now. I moved to a new city, got a new job, made new friends.

Years passed before the fragments and pieces of what I had left behind in Papua New Guinea began to come together again. In that time, I started to talk about what happened in my village, the death of the old man and the killing of the woman. I began to feel I had developed enough perspective to tell the tale the way it deserved to be told.

What I remember of the woman was overshadowed by my concept of who she might have been. In that sense, I made her a ghost, and she had little, if anything, to do with it. The actuality of the woman has long since been replaced by the idea of the *sanguma meri,* the embodiment of innocence destroyed at the hands of desperation. It is the *sanguma meri* that I remember, and it is her that I mourn. I never knew the woman who approached me on that first *wokabout* the day I arrived in the village, who smiled at me and shook my hand. Her suffering ended years ago, and she left it behind with absolute and irrevocable finality. She is finished with that place, but I am not.

And it seems, that place isn't finished with me.

It is not her loss that I lament, or her story that I tell. It should be, but it isn't. We can only tell our own stories and hope by putting them all together their sum will somehow reveal the truth. We examine the parts to try to understand the whole. The moments that make up an epoch.

I try now to remember those moments exactly as I felt them then, to relive the emotions for their sheer intensity and volume. But they're gone, and I remember them now the way I remember my childhood, the day I caught a toad and kept it for an afternoon, cupping it in my hand, feeling its sides pulse with its respiration, the dry warmth of its skin against mine. I can only reassemble images and sensations, piece them together to form an approximation. I can't feel the actual emotions again because they are gone, and the person who felt them is gone, too.

What's left is compressed into instants, memories, thoughts, impressions, and emotions. It's not a few months or two years; it's the blink of an eye, a blur, an instant; so fleeting it scares me, even more as the years continue to pass, because I know now, more than I did then, that this is all there is.

Those months in the village were a confusing and difficult time, and a part of me wanted nothing more than to turn away from what I learned about myself and about my fellow man. But she won't allow me to do that. Too much would be lost; too much remains at stake.

The world today is a different place, a smaller place, than it was even then. In my village, I was removed from the rest of the world in a way that is no longer possible. The machines that so bemused Aha-no have continued to reshape and re-imagine not only the village he loved, but humanity itself. The baffling mechanisms of rampant technology, the disparate concepts of a god, and the greater god—money, have drawn the horizons of our world claustrophobically close. Within the narrow confines of a shrinking world, we eye one another with distrust and contempt. We bump against each other, and when our ignorance or our impatience becomes too much to bear, we explode into violence and destruction, devastating the environs we so jealously guard. But we can no longer turn away from each other–because there is nowhere else to turn.

And so now, more than ever, I find myself dependent on this woman to remind me of the world outside of my own, of the "other," as much as she depends on me to remember her. The two of us need each other, even now, all these years later, as that time and that place fall further and further behind us both, as time goes on, the days turn, and the sun rises and sets, and the rain falls.

That same sun awakens the people of Mari-eka even today, lifting the mists from the ridges and streams as the shadows retreat across the muddied rainforest floor. It warms the air and nourishes the gardens. It fills the people of the villages with a sense of faith and reliance, offering them one of the few certainties upon which they may still depend. They know that even as the sun fades behind the distant mountains this evening, it will emerge again tomorrow, so the day may start anew, and they with it.

I cling to the images of Mari-eka, my Highland village; of the endless and vibrant greenery of the rainforest, the steady drone of insects, the flutter of birds taking wing, the hushed voices of villagers, enshrouded in the morning mist and smoke of their cooking fires, the very scent of life that pervaded the air, the rich, pungent smells of damp soil, blooming fauna, even the decomposition of all that had passed its time. This is the life I remember there, the life I lived there, life in its purest and truest form, without restraint or certainty or even safety. Not the life we try to mask with contrived notions of philosophy or religion. This life is unencumbered with the weight and the confines of what we expect it to be, what we want it to be, or even what we fear it might be. It is filled with a haunting beauty, terrible and exquisite at the same time: terrible because the world inhabited by the people of those villages is as flawed and as fragile and as fallible as the one I had left behind, but exquisite for the same reason; and because of the passion and the elegance and the humanity of those who shared it with me, just for a little while.

What should become of the things we remember?